A Survey of Electronic Cash, Electronic Banking, and Internet Gaming

Financial Crimes Enforcement Network (FinCEN)
U.S. Department of the Treasury
2000

TABLE OF CONTENTS

PREFACE

Since 1995, the Treasury Department's Financial Crimes Enforcement Network (FinCEN) has been examining the potential regulatory and law enforcement implications of emerging technology-driven payment mechanisms, such as smart card and Internet-based electronic cash, electronic banking, and Internet gaming. This initiative was undertaken within the context of FinCEN's mission to support and strengthen domestic and international anti-money laundering efforts.

By developing and maintaining an understanding of how these products work and the role they play within the financial system, FinCEN is better able to make informed judgments with regard to the development of effective anti-money laundering controls. In our pursuit of this goal, we work closely with other U.S. government authorities and maintain a dialogue with key members of the financial services industry. FinCEN's practice is to formulate strategies and programs that minimize the risk of money laundering and other financial crimes, without inhibiting the continued growth of these new payment systems.

In order to share with others some of the findings that have resulted from our efforts in this area, FinCEN has produced this report on *Electronic Cash, Electronic Banking, and Internet Gaming*. The report addresses key commercial developments with regard to these three components of electronic commerce, as well as associated regulatory issues and noteworthy law enforcement actions.

Your comments regarding the content and usefulness of this report are welcome. Any comments or questions may be directed to Shaun W. Lonergan, Special Assistant for Regulatory Program Initiatives, at (202) 354-6416 or by e-mail at loners@fincen.treas.gov. Media inquiries should be made through FinCEN's Office of Communications at (703) 905-3770.

James F. Sloan
Director

FOREWORD

New technology-based payment systems are emerging to present dynamic opportunities for business and consumers alike. Along with these opportunities, however, come challenges for governmental authorities. In rising to meet these challenges, FinCEN, together with other components of the U.S. Department of the Treasury and the Government as a whole, must consider various factors to determine the appropriate course of action to follow with regard to public policy. In assessing the need for anti-money laundering controls, FinCEN takes into account broad issues of financial policy but also recognizes that technology-based products may be susceptible to money laundering and may, therefore, need to be subject to regulatory oversight. The oversight, however, should not impede the continued growth of electronic commerce. Furthermore, while FinCEN's efforts focus on law enforcement and regulatory issues, the agency is sensitive to the need for balancing enforcement interests with those of customer privacy, market independence and other consumer issues.

In this context, FinCEN has been examining the potential regulatory and law enforcement challenges that may result as electronic payment systems continue to grow. This report discusses three distinct types of financial products and services that are technology-based: Electronic Cash, Electronic Banking, and Internet Gaming. Each of these products and services facilitates the electronic transfer of financial value, often in an immediate and secure fashion. These technology-based financial products may also provide a degree of anonymity to the individuals conducting the transactions. For this reason, in addition to providing various benefits for legitimate commerce, these systems may create new vulnerabilities for financial crimes.

The Institute for Technology Assessment (ITA) addressed this point in its October 1997 report *Digital Money: Industry and Public Policy Issues.* According to the ITA report, "Any financial crime—such as embezzlement, insurance fraud, or various cons'—can probably be adapted to digital money. But digital money holds special appeal for money launderers." The report notes that, unlike bulk currency, digital money may be easily concealed, and ITA indicates that some traditional anti-money laundering controls, which were designed to create "choke points" for physical cash transactions, may not be effective in the cyberspace environment.

FinCEN's approach to addressing these issues has been a two-step process: First is education, which is the primary purpose of this report. The nature and operating characteristics of these new financial systems must be understood; to do this, the organization maintains dialogue with members of the financial services industry. FinCEN's first step in advancing this dialogue occurred in September 1995, when it conducted a Cyberpayments Colloquium at the New York University School of Law. The Colloquium brought together financial service providers, software developers, academics, consumer representatives, and regulatory, policy, and law enforcement officials to discuss advances in the design and implementation of emerging electronic payment systems.

Since the Colloquium, FinCEN has continued to deal directly with members of the industry to exchange information and discuss issues of mutual concern. This practice is consistent with the

---

mandate of the National Money Laundering Strategy of 2000, which calls on "The Departments of the Treasury and Justice and the federal financial regulators... to continue outreach to the private sector to ensure that anti-money laundering safeguards respond to new technologies. "

The second component of FinCEN's initiative on new payment technologies deals specifically with money laundering prevention. FinCEN relies upon its knowledge of existing money laundering techniques and methodologies to prevent the misuse of new payment systems for criminal purposes. In May 1996, FinCEN, in cooperation with the National Defense University, hosted a computer-based cyber-money laundering simulation exercise in which participants used advanced decision-making techniques to create hypothetical money laundering scenarios. By drawing upon varied resources for their unique perspective or knowledge, FinCEN hopes to forecast potential new money laundering methodologies and, where possible, to develop preventative measures in cooperation with industry. FinCEN's efforts in this regard continue and thus far have generated a great deal of "thinking outside the box "and new information.

In June of 1997, FinCEN hosted more than 60 senior-level officials from throughout government and industry at a one-day exercise designed to facilitate discussion on the unique regulatory and law enforcement policy issues raised by emerging technology-based payment systems. Among the issues considered at the exercise was the application and effectiveness of existing anti-money laundering controls, such as the Bank Secrecy Act (BSA), in the cyber-space environment. Although consensus was not reached with regard to an appropriate anti-money laundering strategy or specific action items, the participants agreed that the government should be continually evaluating these issues in anticipation that some regulatory and/or other policy actions could become necessary as these payment technologies mature. Since that meeting, as will be discussed in this report, there has been growth in the industry, and there have been regulatory rulings relating to both electronic cash and electronic banking.

Internationally, technology-based payment systems have also received extensive attention. In June, 1996, the G-7 Heads of State called for a cooperative study to investigate the implications of recent technological advances which enable sophisticated methods for making retail electronic payments. Consistent with this objective, a working party was created and it produced a report that developed a broader understanding of the policy issues facing governments as a result of electronic money. In that same year, a new recommendation [No. 13] was added to the Financial Action Task Force's (FATF's) "Forty Recommendations on Money Laundering; "the recommendation states that "countries should pay special attention to money laundering threats inherent in new or developing technologies that may favor anonymity, and take measures, if needed, to prevent their use in money laundering schemes. "During the November 1999 Experts Meeting on Money Laundering Typologies, the FATF continued to focus attention on this issue by conducting specific discussions on the money laundering risks posed by electronic banking.

The Caribbean Financial Action Task Force (CFATF), like the FATF, has begun to consider these issues as well. In May 1998, the CFATF, together with FinCEN and the Commonwealth Secretariat, convened a meeting in Port of Spain, Trinidad, to examine and discuss the implications of these new payment systems. Delegates from more than 25 nations and representatives from various international organizations joined with corporate officials from the financial industry to develop a "Conclusions and Recommendations" paper, which serves as a guide to technology-related policy issues for member governments. In May 1999, the CFATF in cooperation with FinCEN conducted a follow-up seminar on electronic banking and the potential implications for money laundering and financial fraud.

In summary, FinCEN will continue to work through organizations such as the FATF and the CFATF to develop an effective global approach for safeguarding financial systems from the money laundering risks posed by new payment technologies. FinCEN will also maintain its ongoing efforts with the private sector to track industry growth and to raise the level of awareness with regard to new and still emerging technology-based financial services. Finally, FinCEN will continue to work with its various government partners to continually assess U.S. regulatory and law enforcement anti-money laundering programs in order to ensure that the country is prepared to meet any challenges that may be presented by the technology of the 21st century.

INTRODUCTION

The phenomenal growth in the use of personal computers (PCs), fueled in part by the availability of the Internet, has spawned new industries and activities in electronic commerce. More than half of all American households owned a PC at the end of 1998. The public has taken to this electronic technology much faster than it did to radio and television, the technologies of previous eras (see Figure 1). The U.S. Commerce Department reported that American consumers spent $5.3 billion (excluding sales of travel and event tickets) making online purchases during the 1999 Christmas season. More than 50 million households have connected with the Internet in just four years, and many analysts credit technology stocks for keeping the current stock market boom alive. Conventional wisdom says that the future is very bright for electronic commerce.

Every day, businesses and services that traditionally have required face-to-face contact or customer travel to the business site are establishing themselves on the World Wide Web. Bookstores, newspapers, network news organizations, brokerage houses, clothing manufacturers, cosmetics companies, and grocers are establishing websites and selling their diverse goods and services over the Internet. Even those institutions that were once considered the most staid and conservative— banks, savings and loans, thrifts, and credit unions— are making their services available via the Internet to those customers who want to do their banking at home. Furthermore, the entertainment industry is not standing idly on the sidelines during this period of entrepreneurial change: for the first time, the Internet has given gaming (i.e., casino and sports gambling) entre into homes worldwide.

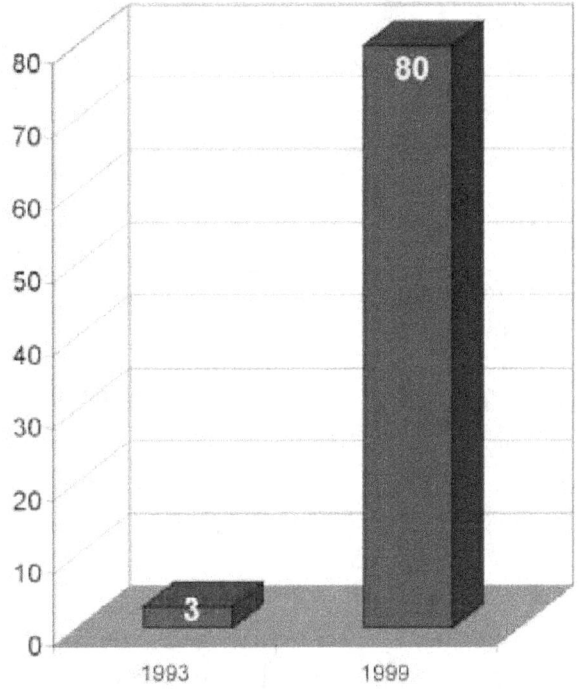

Figure 1
Number of Americans Connected to the Internet, 1993 and 1999, in millions

Source: Based on information obtained from *Washington Post*, "Internet Gets Down to Business," June 20, 1999, A17.

ELECTRONIC CASH

New technology is altering our perception of what may constitute money and is also changing the nature of monetary transfers within the financial system. Electronic cash, or "e-cash," is a digital representation of money and may reside on a "smart card" or on a computer hard drive. Using special readers, stored monetary value is subtracted from the card or, in the case of computer e-cash, monetary value is deducted from the electronic account when a purchase is made. When the monetary value is depleted, the card is either discarded or, in some systems, value is restored using specially equipped machines. Telephone calling cards are the most widely used stored-value smart cards.

Smart cards may also employ microprocessor chips and integrated circuits (ICs). In addition to monetary value, these cards are able to store vast quantities of data in a highly secure manner. This new smart card technology is capable of serving many functions, including credit, debit, security (building or computer access), and storage of medical or other records.

A stored value smart card may be loaded with e-cash in several ways: at a kiosk or a vending machine, at a bank or automated teller machine, via personal computer over the Internet, through use of a hand-held electronic purse or wallet, or through use of a specially equipped telephone (including mobile or cell phones).

Depending on the specifications determined by the issuer, e-cash value stored on a smart card may be transferred between individuals in a peer-to-peer fashion or between consumers and merchants.

Although Americans have not yet taken to the use of stored-value smart cards and/or other types of e-cash, industry experts report relatively wide acceptance of such products in Europe and the Far East. In order to encourage global use of e-cash, analysts point to the need for international standards that make possible inter-operability between systems. Making available multiple applications (that is, stored value, credit, debit, physical security access, Internet payment capability, retail loyalty programs, etc.) on a single smart card would also increase the cards 'acceptance in the global marketplace, according to experts.

As such acceptance grows, many governments and their respective law enforcement and financial oversight authorities recognize their responsibility to carefully monitor technological developments and industry standards in order to prevent the misuse of smart cards and other emerging financial instruments for illicit purposes. Although to date a cautious approach has been favored in most nations, concern about the potential rapidity and anonymity of certain types of e-money transactions has led some governments to consider imposing regulatory controls within the context of their existing anti-money laundering programs.

ELECTRONIC BANKING

Banks have adapted to electronic technology and to the Internet faster than many analysts predicted. Demographic changes (more young people with highly developed techno-logical skills and comfort in using the technol-ogy), combined with low-cost online banking software packages, make PC and Internet banking a dynamic growth area (see Figure 2). According to industry analysts, over 85 per-cent of financial institutions in the United States plan to introduce Internet banking services by the year 2003. The investment

Figure 2
U.S. Adult Population Using the Internet Regularly, 1999

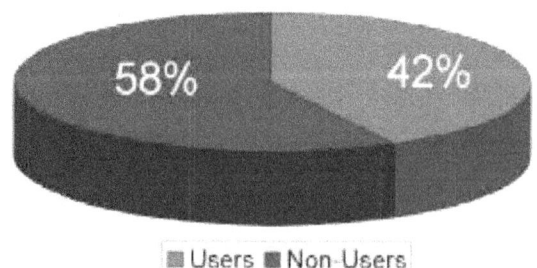

Source: Based on information obtained from *Washington Post*, "Internet Gets Down to Business," June 20, 1999, A17.

banking firm of Goldman-Sachs recently predicted that cyberbanking (Internet-only banks) will make up 20 percent of the banking industry in two to three years.[1]

Whether increases in cyberbanking will result in genuine growth in the industry will depend to a certain extent on the adoption of industry-wide standards. Many of those who attempt to follow the development of electronic banking and accumulate reliable statistics are hindered by confusing or imprecise terminology. Even though the terms *Internet banking*, *web banking*, *PC banking*, and *electronic banking* may refer to different services, banks and consumers often use the terms interchangeably. Some banks, for example, advertise on a bank website but don t actually offer banking transactions via the Internet. Other banks offer PC banking; that is, they offer their customers proprietary software that allows home banking from the customer s computer. Although PC banking is electronic banking, it is not Internet banking. In the latter type of banking, which allows web-based transactions, a bank customer can use any PC that has an Internet connection to conduct banking transactions. True Internet banking allows customers to perform all transactions on the Internet, with the exception of making cash deposits or withdrawals. To comprehend the fundamental difference between PC banking and Internet banking, one need only recall the necessity of direct dial-up connection between the user and the bank (in PC banking) versus the global reach and complete openness of the Internet s world wide web.

Financial regulators and law enforcement officials in many jurisdictions are monitoring with great interest the rapid development of the electronic banking industry. Inadequately regulated or unregulated electronic banking systems may be used to conduct anonymous transactions and to obscure audit trails, acts that may facilitate money laundering and

hinder traditional investigative techniques, especially those requiring the analysis of financial records.

In the United States, electronic banks—whether PC or Internet operations— are subject to the same regulations as brick-and-mortar banks. The same is not true for all jurisdictions, however. Some observers suggest that in order to guard against widespread criminal misuse, international standards for electronic banking should be established by governments as these systems progress and their consumer acceptance increases.

INTERNET GAMING

Another emerging type of technology-based financial activity is Internet gaming (casino gambling, sports betting, and lottery via the Internet). The number of gaming sites on the Internet has grown rapidly in just a few years, rising from approximately six in 1996 to more than 600 in 2000. This growth has attracted the attention of legislators and policy makers worldwide. Officials from various law enforcement agencies have expressed concern that Internet casinos could become venues for money laundering and other types of financial crime, particularly in light of the fact that brick-and-mortar casinos have been used for illegal activities in the past. This potential for criminal misuse is compounded in jurisdictions where Internet gaming is legally permitted but not subject to regulatory oversight.

Discussions regarding the legal status of Internet gaming in the United States are taking place both at the state and the federal level. Most state governments consider virtual gaming sites to be within their domain (as is the case with brick-and-mortar casinos), and, in advance of any new federal legislation, many of them have taken the position that

Internet gaming is illegal under their existing laws. As a result, a number of states have instituted criminal and civil legal proceedings against individual Internet gaming operators. In 1998, 1999, and 2000, bills that would have, in effect, banned Internet gaming were introduced in both the U.S. Senate and the House. No final action on this legislation had been taken as of July, 2000.

This report summarizes the commercial and technological developments and the regulatory policy issues associated with the emerging electronic cash, electronic banking, and Internet gaming industries. As of 2000, all three activities were positioned to continue growing at a rapid pace (see Figure 3). However, lack of standardization in smart card technology, concerns about security risks and lack of privacy in electronic banking, and questions about regulation of Internet gaming may temper the spectacular growth witnessed since 1995.

Growth may come through other developments, however. PCs are only one of many potential Internet transport mechanisms, and technological changes are forecast that could make the PC an Internet dinosaur. Cell telephones (so-called smart cellphones), televisions, connected organizers, Internet pads, and smart telephones fitted with screens and cameras for two-way videos and rudimentary computing powers will allow people easier and more portable access to the Internet. As a result, financial transactions may become more numerous and less dependent upon the physical location of the parties or the intercession of traditional payment methods. The use of mobile phones for Internet banking, for example, is one of the fastest developing trends in Europe and Asia.

However, the concern for personal privacy is rapidly becoming a leading worldwide issue. As people take advantage of being more interconnected through electronic communication, they are increasingly worried about others who may eavesdrop on private electronic conversations, compile databases containing personal information, steal confidential financial data, or destroy private records—either by accident or through malice. Financial information that flies through cyberspace is susceptible to theft and misuse, and until reliable safeguards are established, the fear of the loss of privacy will be present in the public consciousness.

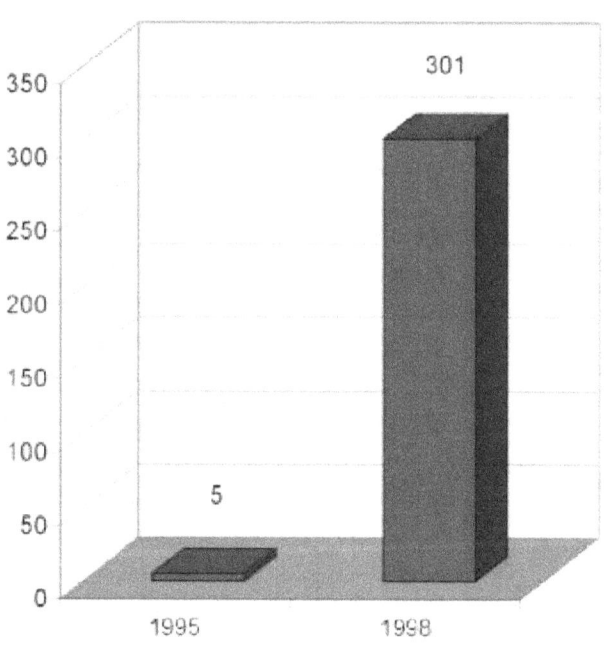

Figure 3
Revenue Generated by the Internet,
1995 and 1998, in billions

Source: Based on information obtained from *Washington Post*, "Internet Gets Down to Business," June 20, 1999, A17.

ELECTRONIC CASH

INTRODUCTION

The terms *electronic cash, e-cash,* or *e-money* refer to electronic payment schemes that enable consumers to store and redeem financial value. They operate via stored electronic units of value. Paid for in advance by conventional money and representing equivalent units in real currency, these funds can be transferred between vendors and individuals using compatible electronic systems, in some cases without resort to banks or other financial intermediaries. E-cash (or e-money) comes in two basic forms: smart card e-cash and computer e-cash.

E-cash is most often downloaded from its respective system through special terminals (for example, specially equipped ATM machines, computers, or cell-phones) onto smart cards. Such cards are called stored-value smart cards. E-cash can also be downloaded to personal computer hard disks via a modem. The "money" remains stored until the user spends it. In the case of smart cards, the "money" is spent by transacting it with another individual, in vending machines, turnstiles, toll-collecting devices, or retailers' terminals. In the case of computer e-cash, the "money" is spent over the Internet. Each e-cash transaction reduces the amount of stored "money" (value).

SMART CARDS/STORED VALUE CARDS

THE BASICS

A smart card consists of a specifically designed integrated circuit chip embedded in a plastic card. The chip contains either a set of contacts that physically connects with an electronic reader or an aerial for contactless operation.

Because they contain one or more electronic chips or integrated circuits that can store and protect information, smart cards are also called chip cards or integrated circuit cards. If, in addition to integrated circuits, a smart card contains a microprocessor chip, it can calculate addition and subtraction of value. The capabilities of their embedded chips are what make smart cards "smart." Many so-called smart cards are, in fact, only memory cards because their chips do not contain a microprocessor. Memory cards can store data and value, but they cannot perform complex calculations. If they are used to store value, as, for example, is the case with telephone cards, they can deduct value only from the total available as the card is used.

Smart cards are to be distinguished from the most common form of card technology for automatic reading—the magnetic stripe card. Based on a much older technology than that used in smart cards, magnetic stripe cards carry encoded information in strips of magnetic tape bonded to a plastic or paper carrier. Because the magnetic coding resides on the outside of the card, the data are vulnerable to tampering. Data can also be erased or corrupted by stray magnetic fields.

Magnetic stripe cards and smart cards also differ as to the amount of data that can be stored on the card. Smart cards can store up to 500 times more data than can a typical magnetic stripe card. They can also store it more securely because of software installed in the chips that is designed to prevent unauthorized usage. Consequently, smart cards offer an attractive alternative to traditional magnetic stripe cards, whether they are used for stored value, debit or credit functions, or for non-financial transactions such as building access or computer access and retail loyalty schemes.

The capability to store value on a card's chip— value that can be expended as well as replenished— is one of the major attributes of smart cards. The simplest stored-value smart card is one with a single store of value issued by a particular company and usable to buy goods and services only from that company (i.e., closed circulation). Such types of cards function almost like a telephone card and are used, for example, in vending machines. When a stored-value card is designed to be used in open circulation (that is, when it is possible to use the card to buy goods and services from several different suppliers), it is termed an *electronic purse*, or *e-purse*.

Because of the limitations associated with card readers, some of which are not able to read card computer chips, smart cards may combine two different technologies on a single card, coming equipped with both a microchip and a magnetic stripe. Known as hybrids, these cards can be read by a variety of readers of differing capabilities. Hybrid smart cards are currently being used to help introduce smart cards to consumers and merchants.

Smart cards have proven much more successful in Europe, and to a lesser extent in Asia, than in the United States (see Table 1). Their success is in part a result of the relatively centralized banking system in Europe, which makes the issuance and servicing of smart cards easier and less costly. In the United States, the banking system, although decentralized, has developed a highly efficient system of automated check processing and has invested extensively in magnetic stripe card technology. This payment system infrastructure makes checks, credit cards, and magnetic stripe cards more attractive and considerably less expensive to process than stored-value smart cards. In addition, the U.S. telecommunications industry is capable of faster, cheaper, and more reliable service than is found in most other countries, including European countries.[2]

STORED-VALUE CARD ISSUERS

In the late 1990s, three stored-value e-cash systems suited to the smart card form— VisaCash, Mondex, and Proton—were prominent in international markets. Various smaller schemes play important roles in restricted markets. Visa International, the world's largest credit card company, introduced VisaCash, its version of smart card e-cash, in 1995. The card is intended to be used for small purchases such as a cup of coffee, a newspaper, a pay phone call, cinema tickets, or public transportation. VisaCash cards store units of prepayment and come in two main types— disposable and reloadable.

Table 1.
Number of Smart Cards in Circulation, 1997

Region	Cards Sold	Market Share
Europe	870,000,000	66.9%
Asia/Pacific	225,000,000	17.3%
Americas	165,000,000	12.7%
Rest of world	40,000,000	3.1%
Total	1,300,000,000	100.0%

Source: Based on information obtained from Card Technology Magazine, *June 1998.*

Figure 4
Smart Card Sales, Selected Years, 1975-1995,
in millions of cards

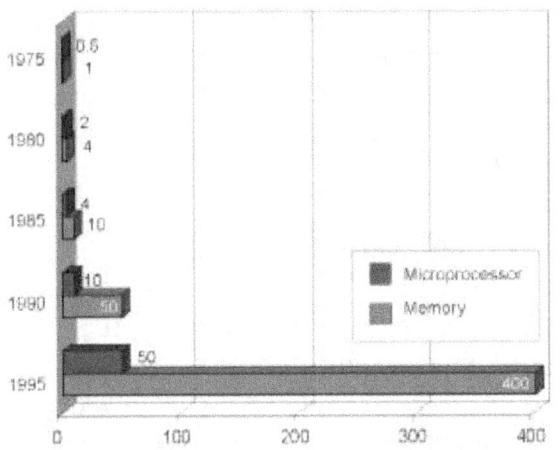

Source: Based on information obtained from Mike Hendry, *Smart Cards Security and Applications*, Boston, 1997, 44.

Disposable cards, loaded with predetermined value, typically come in denominations of local currency, for example, US$10. In 1999, VisaCash disposable cards were available in the United States in $10, $20, $50, and $100 denominations. When the value of the card is used up, the user discards the card and purchases a new one from a card dispensing machine. Reloadable cards, which are issued by banks, come without a predefined value, although in early trials Visa placed an upper limit of $100 on its reloadable cards. When the stored value is used up, the user can load new value onto the card at specialized terminals and ATMs.

Since the mid-1990s, important VisaCash pilots either have been concluded or are currently under way in the United Kingdom, Japan, and the United States. In October 1995, a pilot was undertaken at Visa's headquarters in California. A larger and more widely publicized trial occurred in 1996 at the Summer Olympic Games in Atlanta.

Although results of the Atlanta test were mixed, Visa has also continued with pilots in such locales as Hong Kong; Kobe, Japan; and Leeds, England, where 60,000 VisaCash cards were in circulation during 1998. Visa is also assisting the People's Bank of China to introduce a chip-based payment card called Golden Card. The bank believes two hundred million or more Golden Cards will be in use by 2004. Visa has also supplied the technology for the introduction of smart cards into the bus and rail network in Seoul, South Korea, and, during 1998, launched a VisaCash pilot in Kobe, Japan. By late 1999, about 8 million VisaCash cards had been issued in more than 60 VisaCash programs worldwide.

Mondex, another major smart card e-cash scheme, was created in 1993, when National Westminster Bank in Britain announced development of an electronic low-value payment system to be used for simple, everyday cash transactions. The Mondex microchip contains a "purse" in which Mondex value is held electronically. The purse is divided into five separate pockets, allowing up to five different currencies to be held on the card at any one time. The microchip also contains security programs.

Because the value is electronic, Mondex e-cash can be transferred over a telephone line or the Internet directly to a retailer, business outlet, or an individual, eliminating the need for intermediaries such as banks or other third parties. Thus, the Mondex system eliminates the difficult task of sending cash to remote locations. Although a large amount of value theoretically can be loaded onto a Mondex e-purse card, thus far issuing banks have acted to limit Mondex value. For example, in a current trial in the United Kingdom, an upper limit of electronic value has been set at 500 British pounds (about US$800).

In July 1996, 17 major world financial institutions founded Mondex International; among the founders were its original developer, National Westminster Bank, Midland Bank, Hongkong & Shanghai Banking Corp., Wells Fargo, AT&T, and 10 major banks in Australia and New Zealand. The following November, MasterCard International acquired a majority stake in Mondex and since then has licensed the program worldwide on a regional basis. Mondex International is responsible for managing the Mondex e-purse technology and brand name as well as new product development. Multiple tests are being conducted simultaneously in the United States, China (Hong Kong), New Zealand, Canada, and the United Kingdom. The largest pilots are in the United Kingdom (31,000 cards) and Hong Kong (20,000 cards). MasterCard plans to create a multifunction card using Mondex technology in its credit and debit cards, which total 350 million worldwide. In 1999 there were about two million Mondex-enabled cards in use around the world.

Proton, a third major smart card e-cash scheme, is a rechargeable electronic purse developed by Banksys, a Belgian Electronic Funds Transfer network operator, and is marketed by Belgian banks. Proton is similar to VisaCash in that its value is denominated in units of prepayment; it is likewise intended to be used for low-value purchases from shops or from vending machines. Proton cards can be reloaded at ATMs, payphones, specially equipped home phones, and via the Internet in amounts ranging from 100 to 5,000 Belgian francs (US$3 to US$170).

As of the end of 1999, Proton was involved in five national rollouts. One is located in the Netherlands, where a group of retail banks launched a reloadable smart card chip wallet called Chipknip in October 1995. The national rollout began in October 1996; within two years, more than 12 million cards were in circulation. In addition to functioning as an electronic purse, Chipknip cards can be used for identification, retail loyalty, ticketing, and public transportation. Other rollouts are underway in Australia, Belgium, Sweden, and Switzerland.

In July 1998, Banksys, American Express, Visa International, and ERG, the card manufacturing company, created Proton World International for the purpose of further developing the Proton platform and expanding its use worldwide. American Express, in particular, licenses Proton on a world-wide basis and has undertaken pilot tests of its own, including one with the U.S. Marine Corps. By late 1999, Proton-based systems had been licensed in 18 countries, and more than 30 million Proton cards were in circulation around the world.

Other stored value e-cash schemes include the GeldKarte system in Germany, developed by a group of German banks. Based on the number of cards issued, it is the largest electronic purse system in current use. However, Geldkarte may be used only within Germany. Initial tests were completed in 1996, and as of late 1998, more than 50 million cards had been issued in Germany. In the United States, Touch Technology International has developed a fully featured open electronic purse system that is being tested in Hawaii and France. The computer firm Hewlett Packard has also licensed an electronic purse system, this one developed by SIBS, a Portuguese payment network. Hewlett Packard intends to market the SIBS system internationally, beginning in Spain and Costa Rica.

(For information on smart card technology and security, see Appendix A.)

COMPUTER E-CASH

THE BASICS

Computer e-cash, as noted above, entails the issuance of electronic units or electronic value that can be used for payment in place of currency. Often also called *e-money*, computer e-cash made its appearance, primarily in the United States, in about 1995, and is used in virtual transactions over the Internet. Computer e-cash exists solely in cyberspace; in contrast with currency or smart cards, it does not exist in tangible form.

When using computer e-cash, the customer buys value from an authorized provider, as he would with a smart card. Computer e-cash value, however, is then stored either in the customer's home computer or in a safe online repository. When the funds are spent, the e-cash value is credited to a retailer's e-cash account that must later be transferred to the retailer's regular bank account. Computer e-cash is marketed as an alternative to credit cards for normal Internet transactions.

E-CASH ISSUERS

CyberCash and DigiCash are two examples of early computer e-cash payment systems. CyberCash, which was founded in 1994 in the United States, began offering CyberCoin services in September 1996. CyberCash, Inc. touts CyberCoin as the Internet equivalent of pocket change because payments can be made in increments as small as $.25. The upper limit of value is set at $10. CyberCoin features units of prepayment, as is the case with VisaCash, and operates via software installed in a personal computer. The payment service uses the existing banking network system and does not require the opening of a new account at a specific bank. Because payment by CyberCoin involves the transfer of funds between established bank accounts, such payments can generally be traced without great difficulty. In 1997, in addition to offering CyberCoin and its credit card service, CyberCash, Inc. initiated an electronic check system called PayNow Service.

DigiCash, Inc. was founded in 1989 in the Netherlands. In 1994 DigiCash announced e-Cash, a software-based payments system that allows users to send electronic payments from any personal computer to any other personal computer or work station using any computer network, including the Internet. To use e-Cash, a customer opens a special bank account with a bank that issues it. e-Cash differs from CyberCoin in that e-Cash is electronic value itself and not units of prepayment.

e-Cash is similar to Mondex in that it can be circulated outside existing banking networks. In contrast with Mondex, however, once e-Cash is issued, the amount of expended value cannot be divided into smaller denominations, a feature that discourages continuous transfer. In order to prevent multiple use of electronic value, each value amount of e-Cash is given an encoded serial number (blind signature). When an amount of electronic value is brought to a bank, the serial number is checked. Only when the number has not been previously used can the value be accepted by the bank.

Four banks— three in Europe and one in Australia— currently offer the e-Cash product. In the United States, the only bank to experiment with e-Cash, Mark Twain Bank of St. Louis, Missouri, discontinued the project in September 1998. That same year, DigiCash, Inc. moved from the Netherlands to Palo Alto, California. After filing for bankruptcy in November 1998, DigiCash was sold in August 1999 to eCash Technologies, Inc., of Seattle, Washington, a manufacturer of Internet payment software. eCash Technologies continues to market eCash worldwide, calling it P2P, "person-2-person" Internet payment service.

Other electronic money systems continue to be developed. For example, in November 1999, Confinity, Inc., based in Palo Alto, California, announced its PayPal service, which allows a user to send cash to anyone with an e-mail address. The money is charged to the user's credit card or bank account. It resides in an account maintained by PayPal until the recipient requests payment, which is effected either by check or as a credit to the recipient's credit card or bank account. All payment transactions are made through PayPal's central server, which ensures the security of transactions. Every user is registered by name, and, according to the company, each transaction is traceable.

Confinity is also developing software for a handheld organizer called Palm Pilot that would allow a user to wirelessly beam money from one Palm Pilot to another. Such "beamed" transactions will also go through PayPal's central server. Both Confinity products are intended to make person-to-person payments as easy and convenient as making purchases from on-line businesses. Western Union has announced that it, too, is developing a service to enable individuals to send funds over the Internet.

REGULATORY POLICY

As electronic money has come into use during the 1990s, the question of the need for regulation has arisen. Various U.S. government agencies are tracking developments associated with new electronic payment technologies. Where appropriate, they are evaluating related regulatory policy issues and issuing advisories about possible measures to inhibit the money laundering potential of these payment methods.

Within the Treasury Department, a department-wide effort under the leadership of the Comptroller of the Currency, took an early and wide-ranging look at the issues confronting government by the emerging e-money technologies. The Financial Crimes Enforcement Network (FinCEN), the Secret Service, and other Treasury law enforcement bureaus participated in this effort, examining the potential impact of e-cash systems on the Treasury's law enforcement responsibilities.

In an effort to address consumer concerns arising from the new electronic payment technologies, the Treasury in 1996 organized the Consumer Electronic Payments Task Force. Included in its membership were senior level officials from the Office of the Comptroller of the Currency (OCC), the Board of Governors of the Federal Reserve System, the Federal Deposit Insurance Corporation (FDIC), and the Federal Trade Commission (FTC). According to the task force's report, "the mission of the task force was to identify, in partnership with private industry and the public, consumer issues raised by emerging electronic money technologies and to explore the extent to which innovative responses were being developed that are consistent with the needs of the developing market."

In 1997, the task force held two public hearings and a series of information exchanges with the financial services industry. In April 1998, the task force issued a report on its findings that focused on electronic money products and such issues as access for all consumers, user privacy, and disclosure of consumer rights and responsibilities by issuers. The task force did not recommend new regulation at this time but did foresee a government role in promoting responsible self-regulation by the industry.

The cautious position of U.S. regulators is clear from a speech given by the Comptroller of the Currency in 1996. At a conference on the role of government and electronic money and banking in Washington, D.C., the Comptroller stated, after noting that the public and private sectors should work together wherever possible: "We should avoid premature regulation. We recognize the dangers of involving government too early in such a rapidly evolving area and do not want to chill or unduly influence the market by encumbering it with regulation that may quickly become outmoded, inappropriate, or detrimental." However, he also noted that regulators should be prepared to act when necessary, because "waiting too long to address problems also will impede the full development of this promising market."[3]

The Comptroller's views are clearly representative of those across a wide spectrum of federal government opinion makers. In September 1996, the FDIC issued General Counsel's Opinion Number 8, which addressed the issue of whether stored value represents an insured deposit. Also that month, the agency held a public hearing on stored value and electronic payment systems in which experts explored regulatory issues. Congress has held a series of hearings since 1996 and has explored various issues but has not passed specific legislation.

The most recent regulatory action with regard to electronic cash came in August of 1999, in connection with the Treasury Department's issuance of a final regulation on the application of the Bank Secrecy Act (BSA) to those non-bank financial institutions called "money services businesses" (MSBs). Investigations previously had revealed that certain segments of the MSB industry, which in 1996 accounted for $200 billion in financial transactions, are susceptible to money laundering. As noted by the Treasury Secretary, "Enhancing anti-money laundering requirements for MSBs demonstrates Treasury's firm commitment to close off all avenues used by money launderers to move their illicit funds into the economy."

Included under the rule's definition for MSB's are money transmitters, issuers, redeemers and sellers of money orders, traveler's checks, stored value (electronic cash), check cashing businesses, and currency exchanges. Although issuers, sellers, and redeemers of stored value are defined as MSBs, they, unlike the other types of institutions, are not required to register with FinCEN or to maintain a list of their agents under the final version of the rule. This exemption for electronic cash reflects FinCEN's efforts to strike an appropriate balance between law enforcement's need for accurate information about the owners and locations of MSBs, and the concern that small businesses and developing industries be spared unnecessary and intrusive regulation. Issuers, sellers, and redeemers of electronic cash are, however, subject to certain BSA reporting requirements, including currency reporting in instances of cash transactions exceeding the $10,000 reporting threshold.

Other U.S. government regulators, such as the OCC, have issued guidelines to banks and examiners on the handling of stored value products. For example, in September 1996, the OCC disseminated guidelines on stored value systems to national banks, alerting them to risks and to other issues the banks may need to consider when dealing with such systems. This approach is in keeping with the regulators 'conviction that, at present, it is best to allow the electronic money industry to develop without the hindrance of government regulation.

(For efforts at international regulation of e-cash, see Appendix B.)

SUMMARY OF ELECTRONIC CASH IN THE NEAR TERM

At the end of 1999, an estimated 1.5 to 1.7 billion smart cards were in worldwide circulation. Of this total, 23 million were Visa chip cards, including more than 8 million VisaCash cards. Also in circulation were about 30 million Proton cards and roughly 2 million Mondex cards. Other forms of electronic money worthy of mention were CyberCash and eCash. Both operated via personal computers and the Internet, although they were considerably less significant in terms of volume than chip—based e-purses.

The immediate future of electronic cash was expected to be closely tied to smart cards, the platforms that can carry electronic money on their chips. Although there was general agreement among analysts that smart cards were a viable technology, there was some disagreement about the pace and size of smart card growth.

Datamonitor, a New York firm, predicted in a 1998 report that by 2000 the number of smart cards issued worldwide would number 3.85 billion, most of them phone cards.[4] Datamonitor expected that although Europe would continue as the largest market for smart cards, the most rapid growth would occur in the United States. Growth elsewhere would be concentrated in the Asia/Pacific market, followed by Canada and Latin American nations. The impetus behind smart card growth was expected to be multi-application cards, which Datamonitor predicted would number some 350 million in 2002.

Forrester Research, another American firm, made a more cautious assessment.[5] In a 1998 report of their own, Forrester analysts did not anticipate widespread use of smart cards in the U.S. and Canada until at least the turn of the century, and they expressed little confidence in multi-application smart cards in the immediate future. They predicted that by 2002, card totals might reach 4.7 million, up from 429,000 in 1997. A company spokesman commented that although many people expected the market to explode, Forrester did not foresee that type of growth in the next five years.

Frost & Sullivan, a third U. S. technology research firm based in Mountain View, California, assessed the worldwide smart card market in late 1999.[6] The firm anticipated 29 percent growth for 1999, mostly in the telecommunications industry. Noting some leveling-off of growth while smart card technology moved from the development phase to practical application, Frost & Sullivan, nonetheless, foresaw the number of smart cards rising steadily from 900 million in 1997 to about 3.6 billion in 2002 to perhaps 5.7 billion in 2004 (see Figure 5). Europe would continue to dominate the market, followed by the Asia/Pacific region, Latin America, and North America.

In this country, stored value smart cards are currently limited to a few highly controlled pilots (including "closed systems "such as college campuses), and electronic money barely registers in terms of overall volume of payment transactions. The federal government remains interested, however, in the potential of electronic means of payment. In March 1998, a Presidential panel expressed hope that the U.S. government would be fully committed to electronic commerce within three years.

It unveiled a plan to integrate electronic purchasing tools, including smart cards, with commercial electronic payment processing by 2001.

As early as 1996, the General Services Administration (GSA) took the lead in coordinating an interagency management approach to electronic commerce, including smart cards.

By late 1998, GSA had prepared a set of guidelines designed to ensure that federal agency smart card initiatives would be interoperable and not a hodgepodge of incompatible card programs. The guidelines are intended to encourage those federal agencies with an interest in smart card systems to design them with similar architecture and interface. During 1999 GSA refined the

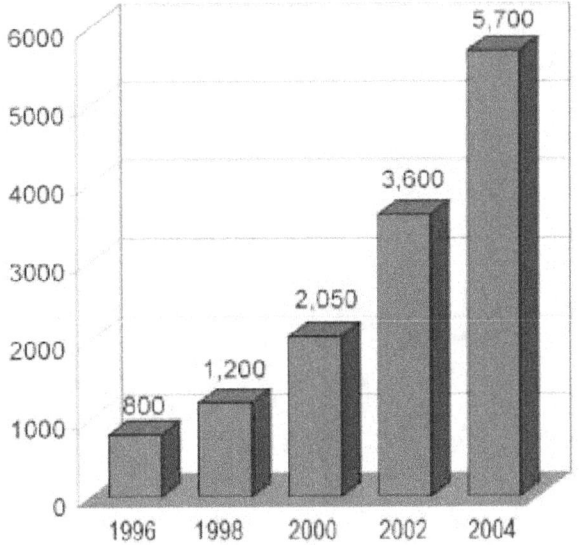

Figure 5
Smart Card Growth, 1996-2004,
in millions of cards per year

Source: Based on information obtained from Frost & Sullivan, "The World Market in Review [1999]." <http://www.smartcardcentral.com>

requirements of what it called its Smart Identification Card, and in early January 2000 released a request for proposals from private vendors to produce it. GSA hopes to have the first multi-application and interoperable Smart Identification Cards in circulation by late 2001.

In the meantime, GSA has instituted a smart card pilot among a group of its own employees. Beginning in May 1999, some 400 employees received multi-application smart cards in a test of the technology. GSA hoped to expand the pilot to include even more employees in 2000.

The GSA pilot and the Smart Identity Card have been of significance beyond U.S. government circles. It is possible that these initiatives may help foster other compatible smart card systems in the United States if, as some industry executives expect, the federal government becomes the catalyst for the introduction of smart cards to the U.S. public.

Whatever the varying assessments of the potential of stored value smart cards and e-cash, at the end of 1999 these industries were still in their infancy. The basic technology was at hand but, according to many analysts, the public acceptance and the broad applications necessary to make smart cards truly viable were still a few years away.

What was certain at the end of the 20th century was that electronic payment schemes and smart cards had arrived on the scene. What was uncertain was how quickly they would be perfected and how quickly they would gain acceptance among consumers.

ELECTRONIC BANKING

INTRODUCTION

Electronic banking is an umbrella term for the process by which a customer may perform banking transactions electronically without visiting a brick-and-mortar institution. This report examines the basic technology and applications of electronic banking, the growth of transactional websites, the geographic distribution of electronic banking activities, the regulatory bodies and instruments connected to electronic banking, fraudulent Internet banking institutions, and the trends and prospects for transactional banking activities. An Appendix to this report provides a list, with websites, of selected Internet banks.

The following terms all refer to one form or another of electronic banking: personal computer (PC) banking, Internet banking, virtual banking, online banking, home banking, remote electronic banking, and phone banking. PC banking and Internet or online banking are the most frequently used designations. It should be noted, however, that the terms used to describe the various types of electronic banking are often used interchangeably.

PC banking is a form of online banking that enables customers to execute bank transactions from a PC via a modem. In most PC banking ventures, the bank offers the customer a proprietary financial software program that allows the customer to perform financial transactions from his or her home computer. The customer then dials into the bank with his or her modem, downloads data, and runs the programs that are resident on the customer's computer. Currently, many banks offer PC banking systems that allow customers to obtain account balances and credit card statements, pay bills, and transfer funds between accounts.

Internet banking, sometimes called online banking, is an outgrowth of PC banking. Internet banking uses the Internet as the delivery channel by which to conduct banking activity, for example, transferring funds, paying bills, viewing checking and savings account balances, paying mortgages, and purchasing financial instruments and certificates of deposit. An Internet banking customer accesses his or her accounts from a browser— software that runs Internet banking programs resident on the bank's World Wide Web server, not on the user's PC. NetBanker defines a 'true Internet bank "as one that provides account balances and some transactional capabilities to retail customers over the World Wide Web. Internet banks are also known as virtual, cyber, net, interactive, or web banks.

To date, more banks have established an advertising presence on the Internet— primarily in the form of informational or interactive websites— than have created transactional websites. However, a number of banks that do not yet offer transactional Internet banking services have indicated on their websites that they will offer such banking activities in the future.

Although Internet banks offer many of the same services as do traditional brick-and-mortar banks, analysts view Internet banking as a means of retaining increasingly sophisticated customers, of developing a new customer base, and of capturing a greater share of depositor assets.[7] A typical Internet bank site specifies the types of transactions offered and provides information about account security. Because Internet banks generally have lower operational and transactional costs than do traditional brick-and-mortar banks, they are often able to offer low-cost checking and high-yield certificates of deposit.

Internet banking is not limited to a physical site; some Internet banks exist without physical branches, for example, Telebank (Arlington, Virginia) and Banknet (UK). Further, in some cases, web banks are not restricted to conducting transactions within national borders and have the ability to make transactions involving large amounts of assets instantaneously.[8]

According to industry analysts, electronic banking provides a variety of attractive possibilities for remote account access, including:

- availability of inquiry and transaction services around the clock;

- worldwide connectivity;

- easy access to transaction data, both recent and historical; and

- "direct customer control of international movement of funds without intermediation of financial institutions in customer's jurisdiction."

TECHNOLOGY

SECURITY

Concerns over security, privacy, and reliability have led consumers to take a cautious approach to electronic banking. Hence, banks seek to assuage customers 'fears about the safety of their Internet financial transactions by providing information about the technology and the safeguards they employ. Banking institutions stress that they provide safe internal operational controls— that is, layered security.

A variety of software packages are available to support electronic banking activities. Internet-based transactions rely on browsers as front-end software. The transactions require three levels of security: first, an encryption standard, either a Secure Electronic Transaction (SET) or a Secure Sockets Layer (SSL) protocol that assures message integrity, allows for the transfer of a digital signature for authentication procedures, and provides confidentiality for the data that flow between a Web server and a browser; second, firewalls and filtering routers; and third, an internal operating system that provides protection for stored information. As an added measure of security, customers are assigned a personal identification number (PIN) and a password for accessing their accounts. SSL provides data encryption and message integrity for an Internet connection; it can also provide server authentication, provided the user knows the steps to authenticate. SSL security protocol on the Web server and customer browser ensures that authenticated data have been received from the customer. Although SSL often involves very strong encryption, the banking industry seems to prefer the SET protocol because SET provides for the authentication of all parties to the transaction and SSL does not.

OPENING AN ACCOUNT

There are several ways to open and fund an electronic banking account in the United States. Customers who have existing accounts at brick-and-mortar banks and want to begin using electronic banking services may simply ask their institution for the software needed for PC banking or obtain a password for Internet banking. Either approach requires minimal paperwork. Once they have joined the system, customers have electronic access to all of their accounts at the bank.

New customers can establish an account either by completing a PC banking application form and mailing it to an institution offering such a service or by accessing a bank's website and applying online for Internet banking. In either instance, the customer can fund the new online account with a check, wire transfer, or other form of remittance. No physical interface between the customer and the institution is required.

GROWTH

Despite concerns about security, reliability, and privacy, electronic banking is positioned for dynamic expansion. Growth of the Internet, consumer comfort with technology, and demographics (younger persons in higher income groups), combined with low-cost PC and Internet banking solutions, have made that expansion inevitable. The former CEO of Bank One Corporation believes that the demographics of Internet use are indicative of the potential expansion of Internet banking. (In only four years, the Internet has reached 50 million households. During the 1998 Christmas season, approximately $8.6 billion in retail goods was sold over the Internet, more than three times higher than predicted.) The former Bank One CEO notes that "there is no banking transaction— other than taking deposits— that can't be done on the Internet. You make all your payments, you get your loans, you get your mortgages. "[9]

INTERNET BANKING WEBSITES AND GROWTH

Websites of banks on the Internet may be either information-only sites or transactional sites. As of late 1999, most bank websites were informational, but of those that offered transactional capabilities, the ability to check account balances and histories, to transfer money between accounts, and to pay bills electronically were the most common offerings. Many banks, however, attempted to advance their standing by *suggesting* unique value or services. A senior analyst with Gomez Advisors noted that in their campaigns to woo customers, banks "will all find ways to describe themselves as being different. "[10] However, over time, and as banks compete for customers, the trend is for these services to lose their uniqueness and to become standard.

Reports on the number of institutions offering Internet banking services vary among government, private, and trade sources. Some of this discrepancy is caused by terminology, in particular, the generic use of the term *electronic banking* and the assumption that the term *Internet banking* refers to a customer's ability to conduct banking on the Internet, even though it may signify nothing more than a bank's establishment of a website. Further, reporting sources often do not specify whether the institutions referred to are banks, thrifts, or credit unions.

Although there appears to be no comprehensive list of Internet banks, a number of sources provide data on Internet banking. However, these sources categorize their data differently, are compiled with varying degrees of thoroughness, and often provide conflicting information. Among others, the following sites provide information on electronic banking:

- The *Bank Rate Monitor* site < http:// www.bankrate.com /bm /news /rev /rev1.asp> on its "Bankrate.com Web site reviews" page provides weekly reviews of U.S. financial institutions 'websites and indicates whether access is by Internet, the institutions ' software, other software, or dial-up network.

The site evaluates Internet banks by website and assesses content, design, and interactivity.

- The *Online Banking Report* < h ttp:// ▪ ▪ ▪ .on linebankingreport.com >, which has webpages for "True Web Banks and Credit Unions "and "100 Largest Web Banks, " lists those institutions that provide account balances and transaction details to retail customers over the Web and includes the institution ́s service provider and the date added. However, the list is not complete, and relies upon banks to submit information if they are not on the list.

- The *AAAdir Directory of Banks, Credit Unions, and Financial Information on the Internet* < h ttp:▪ ▪ ▪ .aaa dr.com > indicates whether or not a bank offers Internet banking and requests that mistakes and omissions be forwarded to the site.

- *Gomez Advisors* < ▪ ▪ ▪ .gom ezad is ors .com > offers an Internet Banker Scorecard that provides information on a given bank ́s website, overall costs except for loans, and the benefits and shortfalls of its services.[11]

Based on the expansion of sales of Internet banking applications, it is expected that Internet banking will continue to increase rapidly. Internet banking surpassed PC banking activity during 1999.[12] Large banking institutions are spending billions of dollars to put customers online. Smaller institutions are also buying packages from software companies to deliver global corporate cash management services via the Internet.[13]

Data on Internet banking have been collected by the Federal Government, particularly the Federal Deposit Insurance Corporation (FDIC) and the Office of the Comptroller of the Currency (OCC). As of

Figure 6
Growth of Transactional Bank and Thrift Web Sites, 1995-1999

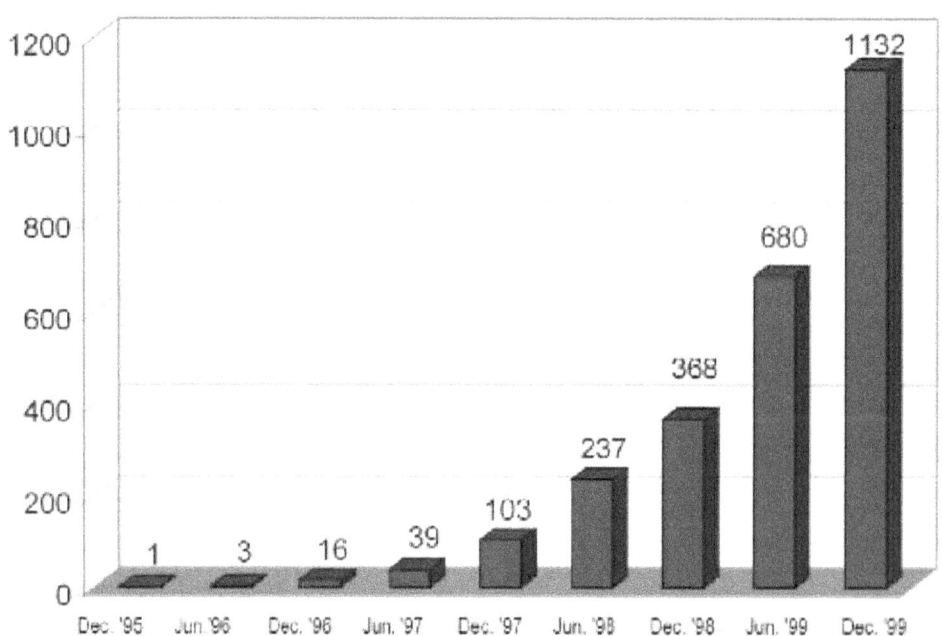

Source: Based on information obtained from: Kori L. Egland, Karen Furst, Daniel E. Nolle, and Douglas Robertson, "Banking over the Internet," *Quarterly Journal,* [OCC] , Vol. 17, No. 4, December 1998, 30, and FDIC data.

late 1999, the FDIC counted 1,132 FDIC-insured banks and thrifts with transactional websites out of a total of approximately 3,500 banks and thrifts with websites. This figure represented an increase from 368 transactional sites a year earlier and from 103 transactional sites in late 1997 (see Figure 6). It also meant that out of about 10,500 federally insured banks and thrifts in late 1999, almost 11 percent offered transactional banking, more than a three-fold increase from late 1998 but still a relatively small percentage of banking activity. FDIC data collection has been enhanced by a June 30, 1999, request that banks and thrifts report their website addresses on their quarterly financial reports.

As of late 1999, at least eight U.S. banks were "branchless" or "Internet-only" banks according to the FDIC. By definition, these banks use the Internet as their primary delivery channel, although some may also maintain a "token" branch office:

- CIBC National Bank < ▼ ▼ ▼ .m arketp lacebank.com >, headquartered in Maitland, Florida, but owned by Canadian Imperial Bank of Commerce; operates on the Internet under the brand-name Marketplace Bank.

- CompuBank < ▼ ▼ ▼ .com pubank.com >, opened for business in late 1998.

- First Internet Bank of Indiana < ▼ ▼ ▼ .firs tib.com > , the only state chartered Internet bank.

- G & L Internet Bank < ▼ ▼ ▼ .glbank.com >, a thrift institution that opened for business in October 1999, in Pensacola, Florida.

- NetB@nk < ▼ ▼ ▼ .netbank.com >, a former subsidiary of Carolina First Bank.

- Principal Bank < ▼ ▼ ▼ .principal.com >, a subsidiary of the Principal Financial Group.

- Security First Network Bank < ▼ ▼ ▼ .s fnb.com >, operated as a U.S. subsidiary of the Royal Bank Financial Group (Canada).

- Telebank < ▼ ▼ ▼ .telebank.com >, one of the earliest true "branchless" banks and a wholly owned subsidiary of E*Trade Group, as of January 2000.

In some cases, traditional brick and mortar banks that have added Internet capabilities have chosen to market their Internet banking product under a different name, which, in some instances, makes it appear as if the Internet function is a separate bank. The following is a list of Internet banks with different names that are actually divisions of FDIC-insured depository institutions as noted:

- BankCaroLine < ▼ ▼ ▼ .bankcaroline.com >, Carolina First Bank, FSB, Traveler's Rest, South Carolina.

- BankDirect < ▼ ▼ ▼ .bankdirect.com >, Texas Capital Bank, Dallas, Texas;

- DirectBanking.com < ▼ ▼ ▼ .directbanking.com >, Salem Five Cents Savings Bank, Salem, Massachusetts.

- Discover Card < ▼ ▼ ▼ .ds cov ercard.com >, Greenwood Trust Co., Wilmington, Delaware.

- Ebank.com < ▼ ▼ ▼ .ebank.com >, Commerce Bank, Atlanta, Georgia.

- EverBank < ▼ ▼ ▼ .ev erbank.com >, Wilmington Savings Fund Society, FSB, Wilmington, Delaware.

- First National Bank of the Internet < ▼ ▼ ▼ .fnbinternet.com >, First National Bank of Cherokee, Woodstock, Georgia.

- Marketplace Bank< ▼ ▼ ▼ .marketplacebank.com > CIBC National Bank, Maitland, Florida; serves as the website for CIBC National Bank.

- Membership B@nking < ▼ ▼ ▼ .americanexpress.com >, American Express Centurion Bank, Oakland, California.

- NBank < ▼ ▼ ▼ .nbank.com >, The First National Bank of Commerce, Commerce, Georgia.

- USAccess Bank < ▼ ▼ ▼ .usaccessbank.com >, Porter Bancorp, Louisville, Kentucky.

- USABanc < ▼ ▼ ▼ .usabanc.com >, Bank Philadelphia, Philadelphia, Pennsylvania.

- WingspanBank < ▼ ▼ ▼ .wingspanbank.com >, First USA Bank (BancOne), Wilmington, Delaware.

(For additional information on selected U.S. Internet banks, see Appendix C.)

Industry sources estimated that, in the second half of 1999, only about 6-7 percent of U. S. households banked online. Online banking, however, holds great potential for businesses as well as for individuals. Among banks offering transactional Internet services, a sizeable number currently offer Internet-based services tailored to business. Such services are likely to become increasingly important to businesses of all size. Industry analysts expect that demand for business services will be another stimulant to growth in Internet banking, which they predict will increase fourfold during the next four to five years.

COST OF SERVICES

Electronic banking, both PC and Internet, costs banks less than does providing services in the traditional brick-and-mortar setting. In 1998, Booz Allen estimated that the cost per banking transaction was:

$1.07	branch service
$0.54	telephone (average)
$0.27	ATM-full service
$0.02	PC banking
$0.01	Internet banking

Other sources, however, point out that the cost of Internet banking is greater than these Booz Allen figures indicate because of the overhead cost of installing and servicing Internet transactions. The true cost possibly ranges from $.07 per transaction to as much as $0.26, according to one estimate.[14] PC banking, because it is a proprietary "dial-up" system serving individualized remote users, is more expensive than Internet banking, which features a centralized system that can reach an expanding number of customers at low incremental cost.

An expert on Internet banking who is affiliated with Grant Thornton LLP, an international accounting and management consulting firm, thinks that Internet software and service providers offer community banks competitive prices for total software and assistance packages that facilitate their entry to Internet banking. He believes that Internet start-up costs are equivalent to the approximate cost of one to two tellers. He views the expansion of Internet banking as providing opportunities to gain market share.[15]

(For a list of selected international Internet banks and websites, see Appendix D. Appendix E discusses Internet banking in different regions of the world.)

REGULATORY OVERSIGHT

The growth of electronic banking has introduced various challenges for financial regulatory officials. Government authorities must continually evaluate commercial developments in order to formulate strategies and programs that minimize the risk for financial fraud and money laundering, without inhibiting the continued growth of the industry.

Today's electronic bank may consist of no more than a computer server and a telecommunications connection and, depending on its location, may be subject to a wide range of regulatory treatment—from very robust and effective programs, to very lax or nonexistent. In addition, an electronic bank whose practices come under suspicion by regulatory and law enforcement authorities may be difficult to investigate because of the remote and global projection capabilities of the Internet and other telecommunications technologies. The victims of a bank fraud and/or the perpetrators of a money-laundering scheme may be half-a-world removed from the physical location of an electronic bank's computer servers. Online payment technologies may also pose other unique problems vis-à-vis concealed transaction identities and insufficient or non-existent audit trails.

Banking supervisory activities and anti-money laundering activities are closely linked in many nations. However, as previously noted, authorities around the globe have widely ranging standards for regulatory oversight and supervision, a factor that may greatly influence their ability to effectively deter money laundering and other financial crimes.

On the positive side, in the mid-1990s, the Institute of International Bankers detected a global trend toward harmonizing supervisory and regulatory standards and noted that "initiatives to increase coordination of regulatory authorities continue to be undertaken, especially through the Basle Committee on Banking Supervision."[16] The Basle Committee, composed of regulatory officials from the major financial nations of the world and headquartered in Basle, Switzerland, issued a report in March 1998, in which it identified some of the risks that banks engaging in electronic banking and electronic money may face. The Committee also considered measures that banks and bank supervisors could take to deal with those risks.[17]

The committee identified three risk categories as most important: operational risks, which involve threats to the security of bank systems or products; legal risks, which may arise from violations of or non-conformance with laws, rules, and regulations; and reputational risks, which result from bank practices or products that may lead to a loss of public confidence. Although none of these basic risks is new in the banking industry, the specific ways in which the risks arise, as well as the magnitude of their impact on banks engaging in electronic banking, may be new for bankers and supervisors alike, the committee warned.

Although the committee dissolved itself after issuing its report, a successor group has been formed to pursue the issue of risk in electronic banking. Chaired by the current U.S. Comptroller of the Currency, this electronic banking group held its initial meeting in November 1999.

FINANCIAL CRIMES ENFORCEMENT NETWORK (FINCEN)

In the U.S., a number of federal agencies oversee the financial activities of the banking sector. FinCEN, under the Department of the

Treasury, is responsible for establishing policy and for overseeing all aspects of Bank Secrecy Act (BSA) compliance by more than 200,000 U.S. bank and non-bank financial institutions, as well as for coordinating federal and state government programs relating to administration and enforcement of the BSA. This authority includes oversight of BSA supervisory, examination, and civil enforcement activities and coordination with federal and state criminal investigators.

Regulations issued by FinCEN require banks and other financial institutions to keep and maintain records, file reports, establish programs to guard against financial crime, and report suspicious transactions to the government. The Suspicious Activity Reporting (SAR) system, which is administered by FinCEN on behalf of the participating agencies, has developed into a primary anti-money laundering mechanism, both in the United States and abroad.

In the context of its responsibilities and authority under the BSA, FinCEN actively monitors the development of the online banking industry. By fully understanding the nature and functional characteristics of banking operations conducted in the Internet environment, FinCEN is better able to determine appropriate BSA program initiatives to prevent money laundering. FinCEN uses written publications and outreach briefings to disseminate information on industry developments and other issues pertaining to regulatory and law enforcement strategies.

FEDERAL FINANCIAL INSTITUTIONS EXAMINATION COUNCIL

The Federal Financial Institutions Examination Council (FFIEC), established in 1979, is a formal "interagency body empowered to prescribe uniform principles, standards, and report forms for the federal examination of financial institutions by the Board of Governors of the Federal Reserve Board, the Federal Deposit Insurance Corporation (FDIC), the National Credit Union Administration (NCUA), the Office of the Comptroller of the Currency (OCC), and the Office of Thrift Supervision (OTS), and to make recommendations to promote uniformity in the supervision of financial institutions." The FFIEC publishes various guides and information booklets for electronic banking. Among these publications is the *FFIEC Information Systems Handbook*, which provides an overview of information systems concepts, practices, FFIEC work programs, and information system controls should be be consulted prior to developing a transactional website.

Another such reference tool for planning, developing, and deploying transactional websites is the *Interagency Guidance on Electronic Financial Services and Consumer Compliance, CEO Memorandum 90*. This publication provides guidance in assessing the implications of some of the emerging electronic technologies for the consumer regulatory environment, an overview of pertinent regulatory issues, and suggestions on how to apply existing consumer laws and regulations to new electronic financial services.

During 1999, U.S. bank regulatory agencies under FFIEC auspices expanded their Information System (IS) examination program to include not only banks and thrifts but also Internet banking vendors. The purpose of the expansion is to improve the security of on-line banking. Currently, the FFIEC IS Subcommittee is coordinating this interagency initiative.

FEDERAL RESERVE SYSTEM

The Federal Reserve System serves as the nation's central bank. The system consists of a seven-member Board of Governors and twelve Federal Reserve Districts located in major U.S. cities. The mission of the Federal Reserve Board (FRB) is to provide the nation with a safer, more flexible, and more stable monetary and financial system. The Board is responsible for conducting the nation's monetary policy; maintaining the stability of the financial system; protecting the credit rights of consumers; and providing certain financial services to the U.S. government, the public, financial institutions, and foreign official institutions. The Board has supervisory and regulatory responsibilities over banks that are members of the Federal Reserve System, bank holding companies, international banking facilities in the U.S., Edge Act and agreement corporations, foreign activities of member banks, and U.S. activities of foreign-owned banks.

In June 1999, commenting on a forthcoming General Accounting Office report on electronic banking, the Chairman of the Federal Reserve wrote that the growth of Internet banking has been fairly gradual, and 'we have not seen significant risks emerge. As Internet services become a more widespread and significant part of banking operations, however, we expect to devote more supervisory resources to examining these activities.'[18] The Federal Reserve has enhanced its monitoring regarding Internet banking and is developing more powerful automation tools in order to aid more generally in examination and review.

FEDERAL DEPOSIT INSURANCE CORPORATION

The Federal Deposit Insurance Corporation (FDIC) is the government agency that insures approximately 10,500 savings institutions, thrifts, and commercial banks. Whether it plans to offer only traditional physical operations, to offer both Internet and physical operations, or to be a fully virtual bank, a start-up institution follows that same application process for Federal Deposit Insurance. Although applications for Internet-based banks are reviewed more carefully with respect to system security and Internet-related aspects of the banks 'business plans, the regulations, laws, and policies for the application process are the same for all banks. A new bank must follow the standard application/approval process in order to obtain FDIC authorization to operate a transactional Internet bank service. Existing banks desiring to add this capability may do so; however, they are subject to review and approval during the FDIC's next examination.

In order to advance efforts to deter fraud and other financial crimes, the FDIC maintains two public information systems, both of which are available through the agency's website. The first system, a computer search engine, allows Internet users to query an FDIC database to determine whether an institution has a legitimate charter and is an FDIC member. All electronic banking and Information Systems information (for example, exam procedures, guidance letters, etc.) is available at <www.fdic.gov/regulations/information/index.html>. From this page, bankers may access all relevant exam procedures, manuals, and official statements, and consumers may access an area that allows them to search for online banks to confirm legitimacy and insured status.

The FDIC also issues Special Alert Financial Institution Letters (FILs) that warn of suspicious banking activities by entities that may be conducting unauthorized banking operations in the United States or abroad. These institutions may be soliciting deposits on the

Internet, offering credit card services, and so on, and may lack both FDIC insurance and a bank charter.

In February 1997, the FDIC was the first federal regulator to develop and issue electronic banking examination procedures and to train its examiners accordingly. The agency maintains an internal program for Electronic Banking Subject Matter Experts, who receive specialized technical training that allows them to perform examinations of more technologically sophisticated institutions.

OFFICE OF THE COMPTROLLER OF THE CURRENCY

The Office of the Comptroller of the Currency (OCC), under the Department of the Treasury, charters, regulates, and supervises national banks, and supervises federally licensed branches and agencies of foreign banks. National banks, that is, banks with the words *national* or *national association* in their title, or the letters *N.A.* or *N.T.* following their titles, represent approximately 28 percent of all insured commercial banks in the United States. They make up about 57 percent of the total assets of the banking system.[19] The OCC supervises more than 2,500 banks.

The OCC is similar to the FDIC in its regulatory process for net banking activities. Under the Bank Service Company Act, a statutory requirement mandates that banks notify the OCC within 30 days if a vendor is providing information technology processing services—that is, an Internet banking package. The law applies equally to the FDIC and the Federal Reserve Board. If the bank is supplying its own technology, it is not required to notify the OCC. New banks such as CompuBank come under the requirements governing the regular licensing process.

The OCC is taking a pro-active stance towards supervising bank use of technology and the risks posed by that technology. The following publications and activities represent some of the measures undertaken by the agency:

Internet Banking Handbook Published in 1999, this handbook provides information to examiners and banks about the risks and examination procedures for Internet Banking. The examination procedures were tested in several examinations prior to publication.

Issuances In recent years, the OCC has issued a broad range of guidance, including:

- Certificate Authority Guidance (BB99-20);
- Infrastructure Threats from Cyber-terrorists (BB99-9);
- Technology Risk Management: PC Banking (BB98-38);
- Technology Risk Management (BB98-3).

Internet Banking Survey To better guide the OCC's activities relating to Internet banking, specialists conducted a survey of the OCC's portfolio managers in the fourth quarter of 1999. The survey indicated that 45 percent of national banks plan to have transactional web sites by the end of 2000. Approximately 90 percent of large banks offer Internet banking today.

Internet Banking Working Group The OCC established this working group to coordinate its multiple efforts to ensure that the agency thoroughly evaluates its Internet licensing, regulation, and supervision responsibilities.

Technical Tools The OCC developed a series of internal technical tools to assist the monitoring of risks pertaining to Internet banking.

The OCC, well aware that technology is changing the banking industry, is reviewing its Bank Information System examination program to keep pace with technology and banks 'growing reliance on vendors and service providers.

OFFICE OF THRIFT SUPERVISION

The Office of Thrift Supervision (OTS), also under the Department of the Treasury, is the primary regulatory agency of all federal and many state-chartered thrift institutions. Such institutions include savings banks and savings and loan associations. OTS regulates approximately 1,120 institutions, and was the federal banking regulatory agency to charter the first pure Internet bank (Security First Bank, in 1995). Since January 1, 1999, the Electronic Operations Rule has allowed U.S. savings and loan institutions to offer their traditional services electronically. This provision authorizes thrifts to use personal computers, the Internet, the World Wide Web, telephones, and automated teller and loan machines to deliver banking services. Thrift institutions that intend to provide electronic banking services must notify the OTS 30 days in advance. The 30-day notice is required for both brick-and-mortar facilities and 'pure "cyberbanks. Thrifts using new electronic technologies must also follow the framework of the interagency Community Reinvestment Act (CRA) regulations and interpretations.[20]

Two reference tools available from OTS for planning, developing, and deploying transactional websites are:

- *Thrift Activities Regulatory Handbook, Information Technology, Section 341* (describes a safety and soundness examination program to evaluate technology risk— useful for planning, deployment, and operation of information systems);

- *Policy Statement on Privacy and Accuracy of Personal Customer information, CEO*

Memorandum 97 (offers information for customers on privacy policies available on websites).

NATIONAL CREDIT UNION ADMINISTRATION

The National Credit Union Administration (NCUA) is an independent federal agency that supervises and insures more than 6,800 federal credit unions and insures almost 4,200 state-chartered credit unions. The NCUA does not require that credit unions submit to a pre-approval and regulatory process for Internet banking activities. However, examiners review such activities during their onsite contacts, which are conducted at least once a year, and evaluate Call Report requirements, which are reviewed at least twice a year. NCUA estimates that about 250 of the approximately 1,700 credit unions with websites offer interactive services.

RECENT REGULATORY DEVELOPMENTS

In March 1999, the U.S. House Banking and Financial Services Committee passed an amendment to H.R.10, requiring that federal banking agencies study banking regulations "regarding the delivery of financial services, including those regulations that may assume that there will be no person-to-person contact during the course of a financial services transaction, and report their recommendations on adapting those existing requirements to online banking and lending. " The regulatory agencies must submit a report to Congress on their findings and conclusions as well as recommendations for legislative or regulatory action deemed appropriate within a year of enactment of the Financial Services Act of 1999. The act was signed into law on November 12, 1999.

In July 1999, the U.S. General Accounting Office submitted a report to Congress that evaluated the efforts of the five regulatory agencies to investigate and supervise Internet banking activities.[21] GAO found that nearly 44 percent of supervised banks had failed to fully implement regulators 'recommendations to reduce risks associated with on-line banking. The GAO report discussed problems specific to supervising Internet banking and made recommendations for improving examination procedures and for limited extension of regulatory authority.

(For Information on International Financial and Regulatory Institutions, see Appendix F.)

CRIMINAL ACTIVITIES

With the global spread of electronic banking comes an increased risk for criminal abuse by those individuals engaged in money laundering, fraud, and other financial crimes. Electronic banks, particularly those operating from traditional 'bank secrecy "jurisdictions, offer many unique services that may be misused for the purpose of laundering illicit funds. However, given that the online banking industry is as yet in the nascent stage, discussion of specific money-laundering scenarios remains hypothetical.

In contrast, investigators have documented that financial fraud, usually perpetrated by an online bank against its customers, is occurring. The fraud often takes the form of unlicensed institutions that accept deposits in violation of federal and/or state law. Both the OCC and the FDIC issue public alerts with regard to financial institutions that are thought to engage in questionable banking activities. For example, the alerts flag institutions not chartered by a recognized regulatory agency, institutions whose deposits are not properly insured by the FDIC, and institutions whose management is not properly bonded to con-

duct such business. Customers are urged to be cautious when depositing funds in flagged institutions. The alerts target both brick-and-mortar and online institutions.

Netware International Bank was the subject of the OCC's Suspicious Transactions Alert 97-14, issued in June 1997. The 'subject entity "was soliciting deposits on the Internet and offering high interest rates. The bank's deposits were not insured by the FDIC, nor had the North Carolina Commissioner of Banking granted the bank a charter. After being advised by the OCC, the FDIC issued Special Alert FIL-71-97, addressing the OCC's concerns. In July 1997, after the execution of a search warrant by the Federal Bureau of Investigation, the bank ceased operations. Netware's officers are being prosecuted for bank fraud, mail fraud, and money laundering in Statesville, North Carolina. In May 1999, guilty pleas were entered in two of three cases— 5:99 CR6 (United States v Bear) and 5:99 CR7 (United States v Skeen). The third case, 98 CR221 (United States v David Bear), was still pending at the end of 1999.

The First Bank of Internet, an entity with a Chicago, Illinois, mailing address, announced in March 1995 that it was initiating transaction processing services for Internet electronic commerce. Despite the use of the term *bank* in its title, the First Bank of Internet was neither chartered nor a lending institution, nor was it covered by FDIC or FSLIC insurance or regulations. Although the bank released a procedures guide with instructions for vendors and customers and provided an e-mail address for verification purposes, in actuality it was a Visa ATM card site used for purchasing transactions over the Internet.[22] The OCC issued an alert warning of unauthorized banking activity by this entity (OCC Alert 95-11) on April 26, 1995. The 'bank "is no longer in business.

The European Union Bank, registered offshore in Antigua and Barbuda, is another bank cited for suspicious activities. Chartered in 1995 with a $1 million investment, the bank collapsed in August 1997. Within one week, the bank had fired all of its employees and its co-founders had disappeared, allegedly absconding with $8 million to $10 million in depositors 'money. The bank touted itself as an Internet institution with private, tax sheltered banking services. The Bank of England and the OCC (Alert 96-40) issued warnings about the bank's operations in October 1996; the FDIC followed in April 1997 (FIL-29-97).[23] The OCC warned that the bank was soliciting deposits on the Internet, was offering high interest rates, lacked the protection of the FDIC, and was operating without authorization, supervision, or regulation by any U.S. financial institutions regulator. The director of the Idaho Department of Finance ordered the bank to cease soliciting deposits from Idaho residents over the Internet, alleging that the bank, which was operating without a state or a federal charter, was illegal. The Antigua and Barbuda government also issued a fraud alert and was seeking the bank's co-founders, reportedly two Russian nationals linked to organized crime.

PROSPECTS

Electronic banking is a growth industry. A flood of "banks"—state banks, community banks, and thrift institutions—as well as businesses and financial investment firms have opened transactional banking sites. International Data Corporation, a research firm, notes that sales of Internet banking applications, including the software to build websites, reached more than $93 million in 1998.[24] International Data projected sales increases of 250 percent in 1999, with Internet banking applications accounting for approximately 33 percent of all U.S. banking applications on the market. The bank consulting firm of Dannenberg and Kellner predicts that Internet banking will become more attractive and more competitive when institutions offering such services expand their distribution systems and offer personal online financial advice over the Internet.

As the industry continues to grow and expand globally, so too will the opportunities for fraud and money laundering, particularly in bank havens and offshore financial services centers. Customers of facilities located in such spots are known to exploit legislative loopholes or banking provisions that facilitate clandestine activity. In the face of this challenge, regulatory authorities have continued to assess their policies, to identify flaws and, as is appropriate, take action to minimize the risk of criminal misuse of the banking system. Given the global nature of the Internet environment, however, this effort must include multilateral consultations among concerned governments if it is to be successful.

INTERNET GAMING

INTRODUCTION

In the last three years, the Internet gaming industry has undergone enormous expansion, going from twelve websites at the beginning of 1997 to an estimated 600-700 sites in early 2000. (For the purpose of this report, the term *Internet gaming* describes web-based casino gambling, sports betting, and lottery operations.) Although the actual amount of current or future gaming conducted via the Internet cannot be measured or predicted easily, experts are confident that upcoming technology improvements and the relative ease of establishing such sites will continue the trend of expansion.

Gaming websites are located in a large number of jurisdictions, including Africa, the Asia/Pacific region, the Caribbean, and Western Europe. In the United States, where gambling regulation has been primarily a state responsibility, there are many proponents of federal legislation that would prohibit the transmission or use of Internet gaming services. Although continued world expansion of this industry is not hard to predict, the legislative process necessary to establish United States policy remained unfinished in mid-2000, and the effort to establish legal controls is ongoing.

This chapter of the report provides information on several aspects of Internet gaming. The first section evaluates the speed at which Internet gaming is growing and factors involved in the development of the commercial market for Internet gaming and the types of financial activity possible using current systems. That discussion is followed by a description of gambling websites as they now exist, emphasizing the types of customers that are targeted and how the sites attempt to deal with obstacles such as customers 'security concerns, legal issues unique to the United States market, and technical problems. The next section discusses the various approaches of national and some regional jurisdictions where there is a current or projected market demand for Internet gaming.

The fourth section discusses recent enforcement actions in the United States, focusing on civil and criminal cases that charge Internet-gaming related misconduct and on recent efforts to establish federal legislation that criminalizes Internet gaming. The final section of the chapter examines the prospects of Internet gaming based on the conditions described in the preceding sections.

COMMERCIAL DEVELOPMENT TRENDS

The rate of growth of Internet gaming is a matter of speculation, as is the total amount of money spent per year. The number of gaming sites also is a matter of speculation: most current estimates range between 300 and 700, with new sites appearing constantly and others going out of business. (Rolling Good Times Online, a source of such information, reported 282 individual sites accepting real-money wagers in February 1999.) According to reports, sites may be established with relatively low capitalization for equipment, software, setup, and maintenance expenses. However, final startup costs depend on the amount required for licensing and bonding by the jurisdiction in question. Once a site is in operation, it must achieve a relatively high volume of gaming transactions to make a profit.

One gaming expert estimates that $10 must be wagered for every $1 of revenue realized by an Internet gaming operator.

PARTICIPANTS

According to the former chair of the Interactive Gaming Council (IGC), the growth of Internet gaming has been fueled mainly by the work of young computer and marketing specialists interested in applying their technology in a high-risk venture with some prospects of profitability. However, larger software and electronics companies, many of which have connections to other, more conventional parts of the computer and telecommunications industries, are playing an increasing behind-the-scenes role in the Internet gaming industry. The character and long-term prospects of this role are not clear. Some of those companies sell gaming systems outright to gaming operators; others take an ongoing percentage-licensing fee. According to the former IGC chair, the number of companies with such involvement has grown slowly but steadily, with most companies appearing to maintain the balance of their activity in jurisdictions with more established financial regulatory programs until governments set firmer national policies.

GROWTH

Estimates of the total amount of business done annually by the industry range from $6 billion to $60 billion. $10 billion has been cited by one industry analyst as the most accurate estimate for 2000. A complicating factor in gauging the growth of Internet gaming is the uncertain legal status of the industry (especially as it relates to the United States), which may have caused many operators to conceal their financial situation and sometimes their identity. The overall lack of clear regulation also makes

it difficult to determine how many enterprises are entering the field and how many are folding. For example, Antigua, which boasts of its strict licensing regime, has issued a list of seven or eight unlicensed gaming websites that were operating from Antigua in 1998. Further complicating matters is the frequent ownership or licensing (the relationship often is not clear) of multiple sites by the same corporate entity and the tendency to change site names or use variations of the same name in different levels of advertising. Online casino and sportsbook listings often give both the parent and the subsidiaries the same status, and often both levels have websites that seem to represent a single casino or sportsbook. An example is Casino Fortune of Trinidad, which apparently went from being a single casino to being the corporate name of several casinos, including one in Botswana, owned by a company called the Sunny Group. Meanwhile, Casino Fortune maintains a separate gaming website exactly like the other casinos.

About 15 companies develop and sell turnkey interactive gaming software for Internet gaming operations. Their number is growing slowly but constantly. According to an IGC expert, the largest volume of such sales has been produced by Atlantic International Entertainment, Inc. and Microgames. Other major players are Cyberoad of Canada, Casino World Holdings of Antigua, CyberSpace Casino Tech and Handa Lopez of California, and Cryptologic of Vancouver. However, some gaming operators have established relationships with more conventional software companies such as Electronic Data Systems Corporation, the supplier of Global Internet Corporation, a Dominica-based Internet operator.

Whatever the growth rate or current level of activity, it is certain that since 1997, those depending on the U.S. market have been substantially slowed by the uncertain legal status of Internet gaming operations in the United States. Major supplier companies such as Virtual Gaming of Antigua and GLC (formerly Gaming Lottery Corporation) of Gibraltar have formally declared that they will avoid direct contact with the American market as long as state and federal laws are interpreted as prohibiting the offering of Internet gaming services in U.S. jurisdictions. Australia's largest online operation, Centrebet, terminated all U.S. commerce in 1998.

SITE LOCATION

The number of countries currently licensing Internet gaming also is a matter of speculation. One industry analyst estimated 20 such countries in November 1998. Among those known to offer some form of licensing are Antigua, Australia, Austria, the Bahamas, Belize, Costa Rica, Dominica, the Dominican Republic, Ecuador, Gibraltar, Grenada, the Netherlands Antilles, St. Kitts, and Venezuela. However, the definition of "licensing" also differs by jurisdiction.

Observers of the industry have pointed out that websites often label themselves licensed by virtue of holding only a general license to conduct business, as opposed to a specific license for Internet gaming. The latter license may not be granted in jurisdictions such as Costa Rica and Venezuela, even though Internet gaming operations apparently are based in both countries. In addition, many casinos operate in countries that do not license Internet gaming. The choice of a site location for Internet gaming may have nothing to do with whether or not a country licenses the operations.

FINANCIAL OPERATIONS

An important marketing tool for the Internet gaming industry is the ability to transfer money quickly, inexpensively, and securely—attributes that conventional casinos, lotteries, and sports betting venues offer to their customers. A person who enters an interactive gaming website wishing to place a bet first must register and deposit a prescribed minimum amount of money (most often $300) with which to establish an account. The conventional ways of placing that money are (1) providing the number of a credit card from which a cash advance is taken and transferred to the casino operator, (2) sending a check or money order, or (3) sending a wire transfer or other remittance of funds. The bettor is able to gamble at the website only when the account has been established. As the bettor gambles, money is added to or subtracted from the initial amount. The bettor may request that a check be sent for the remaining balance at any time; most operators guarantee a short turnaround for this service.

According to one Internet gaming analyst, the conventional methods of transfer have impeded the growth of the industry because they do not provide enough security (a large sum must be forwarded or a credit card number revealed), speed (the transfer of funds via wire or other remittance system takes time), or anonymity (personal information, especially age, also is required to establish an account). There is, in fact, a substantial record of shadow websites collecting such deposits for a period of time and then disappearing, in the process destroying consumer confidence.

He notes that, although money order, check, and credit card transactions still are the most frequently used payment methods for establishing accounts, several more efficient methods of cash transfer are either on the horizon or already in limited use. These include stored-value smart cards, which can store digital information about an account, and electronic cash (e-cash). These new payment mechanisms have the advantages of security and speed. However, at present, high transfer fees make digital cash impractical for the interactive gaming industry. Another problem is that several varieties of digital cash are competing for the market, creating a situation where a prospective bettor's home computer might be equipped for a type of digital cash incompatible with a given gaming website.

Theoretically, as these problems are overcome, a consumer will be able to use e-cash across a wide range of purchases; this marketing approach is being taken by both the provider companies and the gaming companies that offer e-cash as a payment option. At present, however, a relatively small percentage of the Internet gaming community is connected to an e-cash system. When gaming establishments offer account establishment via conventional credit card within a five-minute period, the additional speed of e-cash does not seem to be a great advantage even though the security and anonymity of the technology may prove more attractive.

GAMING WEBSITES

DESIGN AND STRUCTURE

Gaming websites vary enormously in size and structure. Some are simple three-page sites with no additional links, and some are elaborate (and often repetitive) collections of ten or more links and sublinks. Most home pages offer a menu of links. The most common listings are:

- "About Us " (which may or may not contain information about the workings of the company);

- "Contact Us " (usually one or more email addresses with assurance that someone will be available to address problems);

- "Frequently Asked Questions " (mostly about how to deal with transmission and software glitches, often also addressing legal issues associated with the questioner's location);

- "Help " (a list of solutions to possible financial and payment problems);

- "Rules " (sometimes a general statement of how games are to be played and money handled, sometimes a detailed description of how each game is to be played); and

- "Security "or "Security Features " (a list of ways in which a betting transaction with this website will be expedited and protected).

LEGAL ISSUES

The question "Is gambling on the Internet legal? "brings a variety of responses; some sites simply fail to ask it. Some sites, such as Global Sports in Costa Rica, say that the only jurisdiction that counts is the one where the site is located; since they are licensed in Costa Rica, for example, Global Sports maintains that gambling is legal no matter where the customer is sitting. Some sites warn the customer to check local laws before entering. A few list states such as Indiana and Minnesota as jurisdictions where Internet gaming has been declared illegal. And many simply say that the status of a patron's Internet gaming activity is a complex problem that has not been decided definitely or consistently. The question of taxability of winnings is addressed by about half of the sites, often with the answer that no accounting of winnings goes to any customer's government, and that it is the customer's responsibility to determine tax requirements and to comply with them. In any case, it is clear that customers cannot and should not rely on site operators for complete and accurate legal guidance.

LICENSING QUESTIONS

The subject of licensing and specific regulatory requirements is omitted entirely on many gaming websites, and in some cases there is no mention of ownership or location. When licensing is mentioned, the terminology differs somewhat. Some sites state the case directly and briefly (for example, "Casino Money is fully licensed by the government of Venezuela.") In a few cases, there is mention of bonding, periodic monitoring, or other regulatory activity. In other cases, the issue of licensing and location becomes split, as in "Casino Money is a fully licensed sportsbook operating in Venezuela," a construction that may indicate that the location and the licensing jurisdiction are not the same. Compare the more specific statement, "Casino Money is fully licensed by and operating in Venezuela."

According to several websites that comment regularly on Internet gaming, the term *license* is commonly used by the gaming business to bolster its credibility and authenticity to would-be customers. In some jurisdictions, such as Australia, advertisement of a license is indicative that background checks have been made, that a special fee has been paid, and that the business is subject to periodic monitoring and auditing. In other jurisdictions such may not be the case. The term *license* may indicate that a franchise has been issued to the operator by a software and electronics firm that supplies it. In other words, the business is licensed by another firm but not necessarily by a government entity.

SITE SECURITY AND TRANSACTIONS

Also prominent in many (but not all) websites are efforts to reassure the customer of the security and reliability of gambling at that site. In 1998 the Bettorsworld website listed about twenty online casinos and sportsbooks that were reported not to be paying out winnings or to be chronically late in paying. The motivation of such a list may be suspect. However, other sources also indicate that a large number of gaming websites are of the fly-by-night variety. A fair number on Bettorsworld's list still have websites and presumably still take bets. Because even the reportedly reputable Bettorsworld cannot be relied upon to provide information as to the current status of some sites, gaming enterprises make every effort to reassure the potential customer.

Nearly all sites go into substantial detail about how financial transactions are handled, usually offering a wide variety of ways to transmit money to open an account. Methods for the collection of winnings are prominently mentioned, as are encryption systems designed to improve the security of credit card use. Most sites claim to have the most exciting games, the most sophisticated software, and the most customers. Many sites also offer play for fun (especially recommended by some sites for U.S. customers who live in states that prohibit gambling for money).

According to one industry analyst, the technological level of most interactive gaming sites still is far below the expectations of Americans accustomed to efficient television and telephone transmission. Despite the advertising emphasis on the "virtual experience of gambling in your own home," game play often is slowed by long image downloading processes and frequent computer crashes; the system works only as well as its least-efficient link, which often is the user's own PC. And there still is no reliable way for a customer to be sure he or she will not be cheated by rigged games or nonpayment of winnings, will not be breaking some law, or will not have a credit-card number misused.

DEVELOPMENTS IN THE UNITED STATES

Throughout its history, gambling regulation in the United States has been the province of state governments. As such, the range of legal gaming activity in the states is quite varied. Only two states—Hawaii and Utah— prohibit gambling altogether. The other states permit an array of legalized activities, ranging from bingo, lottery, and race wagering, to full-scale casino gambling. In addition, under authority granted by the Indian Gaming Regulatory Act of 1988, native American tribes have established casinos, lotteries, and bingo halls on tribal land in approximately 30 states. In total, more than 500 casinos exist in the United States today.

FEDERAL LEGISLATION

After two years of research into all aspects of gambling in the United States, the congressionally mandated National Gambling Impact Study Commission issued its final report in June 1999. The commission's recommendations on Internet gaming include the following:

- that the federal government prohibit all Internet gambling that is not already explicitly permitted; that the United States Department of Justice develop enforcement strategies against Internet service providers, credit card providers, money transfer agencies, makers of wireless communications systems, and "others who intentionally or unintentionally facilitate Internet gambling transactions";

- that legislation be developed to prohibit wire transfers to known Internet gambling sites or to banks that handle their accounts;

- that any credit card debts incurred in Internet gambling be made legally unrecoverable;

- and that "the federal government take steps to encourage or enable foreign governments not to permit Internet gambling organizations that prey on U.S. citizens."

The Internet Gambling Prohibition Act was first introduced by Senator John Kyl (R-AZ) in March 1997. The 1997 Kyl Bill would have amended the Interstate Wire Act of 1961, which prohibits the use of telephone and telegraph communications facilities for the placing of bets on sporting events. The amendment would include the Internet, which did not exist in 1961, among the forbidden media. The final version of the legislation subjected individual Internet bettors as well as Internet gaming entrepreneurs to a fine and/or prison.

The Kyl Bill was passed by the Senate by a vote of 90 to 10 in July 1998. However, the companion House bill, introduced by Congressman Bill McCollum (R-FL), did not reach the House floor for a vote before the congressional session ended in the fall of 1998.

In March 1999, Senator Kyl introduced a new Internet gaming bill that was substantially similar to the 1998 version. Unlike the earlier version, the new bill does not make placing a bet via the Internet a federal crime; it provides exceptions for fantasy sports, parimutuel betting, state lotteries, gaming activities permitted by the Indian Gaming Regulatory Act and by agreements between states and Indian tribes based on that law, and legally placed bets on horse races. The bill also provides federal authorities injunctive powers to shut down web sites; and it requires gaming companies to comply with state licensing and enforcement standards.

In June 1999, the Senate Judiciary Committee approved the 1999 version of the Internet Gaming Law by a vote of 16-1, sending it to the Senate floor for consideration. The bill calls for up to four years imprisonment and up to $20,000 in fines for operators of online casinos and sportsbooks, and it would extend the provisions of the Federal Wire Act to cover gambling on the Internet as well as by telephone and wire. On November 19, 1999, by a unanimous vote, the Internet Gaming Prohibition Act passed the Senate just prior to the start of the Congressional holiday recess, but the House has not yet passed any comparable legislation.

In April 1999, Congressmen Bob Goodlatte (R-VA) and Frank LoBiondo (R-NJ) announced that they would introduce their bill in the House of Representatives after the National Gambling Impact Study Commission issued its final report in June 1999. On November 3, the House Judiciary Committee's Subcommittee on Crime approved the Internet Gambling Prohibition Act introduced by Congressman Goodlatte and five cosponsors. However, the bill was defeated in the full House on July 17, 2000, falling 25 votes short of the two-thirds majority necessary for passage. Following the defeat, Goodlatte indicated that he intended to continue seeking passage of the legislation before the end of the current session of Congress in December. If he fails, the bill would have to start again with committee hearings in the next session of Congress.

Another piece of legislation, the Internet Gambling Funding Prohibition Act, was introduced in the House of Representatives on May 10, 2000. This new bill would prohibit the use of credit and debit cards, checks, bank drafts, and electronic transfers to place bets, collect winnings, or otherwise conduct gambling activities on the Internet. On June 28, 2000, the bill was approved by the House Banking Committee and, as of August 10, was awaiting further action.

FINCEN SURVEY OF STATE LEGISLATION

Early in 1999, FinCEN sent a survey to the offices of the attorneys general of all the states and United States territories and the Office of the Corporation Council of the District of Columbia. The survey posed three questions related to the jurisdictions 'policy toward Internet gaming:

- whether the jurisdiction has statutes or regulations dealing with gaming in general and, if so, whether any of them might apply to Internet gaming;

- whether any existing or future statutes of the jurisdiction apply specifically to Internet gaming;

- whether the jurisdiction had pursued any criminal or civil actions pertaining to Internet gaming.

Responses were received from 19 states, the District of Columbia, and Guam.[25]

Responses to the question of applicability of current laws or regulations to Internet gaming overwhelmingly expressed the opinion that laws designed for conventional gambling could be interpreted to apply to Internet gaming, depending on the circumstances of a particular case. The criterion most often cited is legal establishment that Internet gaming actually occurs within the boundaries of the state in which the gambler is physically located.

Although no responding jurisdiction cited a law or regulation specifically enacted to address Internet gaming, one section of the Nevada Gaming Control Act lists the Internet as a "medium of communication," giving the State Gaming Control Board official jurisdiction over Internet gaming. In New Jersey, an article of the state constitution says that any new form of gaming must be approved by referendum before being legalized. Therefore, according to the spokesperson for the state attorney general's office, the current interpretation of that article makes Internet gaming illegal. Ohio's interpretation is that any form of gambling that is illegal by state law in conventional form also is a violation of state law when it is disseminated in the state via a computer system. The Alabama Attorney General's office interprets the definition of gambling devices in the state code— "any device, machine, paraphernalia, or equipment that is normally used or usable in the playing phases of any gambling activity"—as including Internet equipment. The interpretation implicitly includes the Internet under the state laws prohibiting conventional forms of gambling.

Alabama has taken no criminal or civil action against Internet gaming, but the decision in a 1999 criminal case, brought for possession of obscene material for transmission via the Internet, rejected the defense that the relevant law preceded the development of the Internet and therefore was not applicable. In Arizona and Tennessee, the authority to prosecute such cases rests with local and district prosecutors, respectively, rather than the state's attorney general.

FEDERAL CIVIL AND CRIMINAL CASES

In March 1998, the United States Attorney for the Southern District of New York indicted 21 U.S. citizens for conspiracy to transmit bets and wagers on sporting events via the Internet, in violation of the Interstate Wire Act of 1961. At that time, the U.S. Attorney General issued a statement indicating that Internet gaming would be considered illegal under existing federal law.

The defendants were owners, operators, and managers of nine offshore sports betting companies based in Curaçao, Costa Rica, the Dominican Republic, and Antigua, all of whom had conducted some part of their business in the United States. All were identified after federal agents placed telephone bets via an 800 number from New York (territory where such bets are illegal) and were paid when successful. One defendant, the president of SDP Global of Costa Rica, pled guilty and promised to pay a fine of $750,000 and close his operation. As of February 2000, ten other defendants had pled guilty to the charges and reached settlements, and six remained officially fugitives because they had not answered the charges. As of that date, only one defendant, Jay Cohen, had gone to trial. On February 28, 2000, the United States District Court in Manhattan found Cohen, the owner of the Antigua-licensed World Sports Exchange, guilty of violating the Federal Wire Act.

Indian Gaming Regulatory Act (IGRA)

As some states were testing how the Indian Internet lottery fit with state law, a case at the federal level was expected to eventually determine whether Indian tribes have special status that allows them to use long-distance telephone lines and the Internet to transmit the lottery to customers in the 33 states where lotteries are legal. In 1997 the Coeur d'Alene Tribal Court in Idaho ruled that the federal Indian Gaming Regulatory Act (IGRA) protected the tribe's lottery from interference by state legal authorities and that long-distance telephone companies could not refuse 800 service by citing the 1961 Wire Act or state laws. (The tribe also argued that long-distance and Internet communication were needed because their distance from population centers presented a competitive disadvantage.) AT&T, the company chosen to provide this service, found itself caught between the tribal court decision, violation of which could lead to a contempt citation, and the possibility that supplying an 800 number would lead to criminal prosecution by states whose attorneys general had advised that such service would be considered a violation of state law. In August 1997, AT&T sought declaratory relief in federal court.

In December 1998, the United States District Court for the District of Idaho denied a complaint brought by the Coeur d'Alene Indian tribe against AT&T for having refused the tribe an 800 number to be used by customers playing its National Indian Lottery. The court ruled that the tribal court ruling did not require AT&T to supply an 800 number in any state where transmission of gaming activities would violate state law. In such states, a separate agreement must be reached to address the state's regulatory interests before the lottery can be offered.

The special status granted by the IGRA was ruled to apply only to gaming activities physically located on the reservation, a line of reasoning that caused the closing of both the telephone and Internet phases of the lottery, although the ruling itself applied only to telephone lines. If the lottery is deemed not to be entirely operated on tribal lands, the Internet phase is open to criminal prosecution by receiving states in the same way that offshore websites with some operations in the

United States have been prosecuted. The tribe appealed the decision to the United States Ninth Circuit Court, which remanded the case to a Missouri state court in September 1999. Argument of the tribe's legal standing continued in that court into 2000.

STATE CIVIL AND CRIMINAL CASES

Several states have taken legal action against individuals and companies that have offered offshore Internet gaming services to individuals within the state jurisdiction. Authorities have initiated civil and criminal cases, issued official policy statements, and sought to restrict transmission in other ways. The following discussion is a summary of some of the state actions to date.

Florida

In December 1997, the Attorney General of the State of Florida signed an agreement with Western Union to the effect that the latter company cease providing Quick Pay money transfer services from Florida residents to known offshore gaming establishments. Quick Pay is a reduced-fee system normally used to expedite collection of debts or payment for goods. According to the Florida State Attorney General and a Western Union spokesman, in 1998 the policy of Quick-Pay restriction yielded satisfactory results, and the prohibition of the use of Quick Pay accounts for gaming purposes was upheld in the federal court case *Cheyenne Sales Limited v. Western Union Financial Services International.* No known website, however, includes mention of the restriction on the use of Western Union services by Florida residents.

The state also was able to persuade the media to stop advertising offshore gaming sites. Florida contended that the advertising of such sites in the state constitutes doing business in the state and invokes all the legal restrictions inherent in aiding and abetting such activity. In this case, those restrictions include the placing of illegal bets (i.e. a form of gambling not specifically permitted by law), which is a misdemeanor, and running a betting operation, which is a third-degree felony.

Indiana

In 1998 Indiana's Attorney General issued a policy statement on Internet gaming. The statement was in response to concerns expressed by the Indiana Commissioner of Higher Education about the proliferation of gambling on college campuses. The Attorney General noted that Indiana law prohibits all forms of gaming that are not specifically permitted, i.e. river boat gambling, pari-mutuel betting on horse races, charitable gambling, and the state lottery. He further asserted that a person placing a bet from Indiana with an offshore gaming establishment was engaged in in-state gambling just as if the person engaged in conventional gambling. He then concluded that the solicitation and acceptance of wagers are subject to prosecution under Indiana state law.

Following the statement, the Attorney General's office sent email messages to more than 100 offshore Internet gaming operators demanding that they cease offering their services in the state and that they post a warning on their websites that using them is illegal for Indiana residents. (Two such warnings have been discovered, on the sites of 123 Casino and Sportsbook in Grenada, and AAA Casino, whose location is unknown.) According to the Attorney General, the main reason for his warning was to bring attention to the danger of exposing minors to Internet gaming, not to enforce a given law.

As of March 1999, Indiana had not developed a policy regarding criminal sanctions against Internet gaming enterprises offering their services in the state.

Maryland

In 1997 the Office of the Attorney General of Maryland reached an out-of-court agreement with RealTIME, which offered Internet games of chance to users and whose equipment was located in Maryland. RealTIME, which had argued that it should not be prosecuted in Maryland because it was not offering gambling to residents of Maryland, agreed to cease its operations in Maryland.

Minnesota

In 1997 the Attorney General of Minnesota brought suit against Granite Gate Resorts, a Nevada corporation, and its president, Kerry Rogers, based on the defendants 'operation of a Belize-based Internet sports betting operation. The lawsuit alleged that Granite Gate and Rogers engaged in deceptive trade practices, false advertising, and consumer fraud by offering Minnesotans access to sports betting. Such betting is illegal under state law.

The trial and appellate courts rejected the defendants 'argument that Minnesota courts lacked jurisdiction because the defendants had merely placed information on the Internet and Minnesotans had chosen to access it. The appellate court concluded that 'Granite Gate's advertising had an effect in Minnesota, that the effect was intended, and furthermore that Internet advertising is not different from other advertising forms such as telephone solicitation or radio advertising. "Minnesota courts had previously concluded that such advertising allowed sufficient contacts with potential customers to establish personal jurisdiction. The Minnesota Supreme Court affirmed the appellate court's decision in April 1999.

Missouri

In April 1997, the State of Missouri brought a civil suit against Interactive Gaming and Communications of Pennsylvania, which ran the Sports International Internet sports betting establishment of Antigua, and against its chief executive officer, Michael Simone. As in Minnesota, the case was based on state consumer law. The case was initiated when a state law enforcement agent saw an advertisement for the sports betting website and placed a wager over the company's 800 number, which was located in Pennsylvania. As a result of the state's civil case, a restraining order and fine were issued. A second wager, placed after the restraining order, led to a June 1997 criminal indictment against Interactive Gaming and Communications for promoting gambling by allowing Internet bets of more than $100. Simone eventually pled guilty to a lesser charge and was fined.

Consistent with its position that state law prohibits Internet gaming, Missouri also sought a permanent injunction against the Internet lottery run by the Coeur d'Alene Indian Tribe of Idaho. The case was removed to the federal level, where in 1999 the United States Court of Appeals rejected a district court decision that the lottery was protected by the 1988 Indian Gaming Regulation Act. The court held that the lottery would be protected only if the gaming occurred on Indian lands. At the direction of the Court of Appeals, the case has been remanded for a decision on the legal location of the lottery, which would be the basis of a final decision.

New York

In October 1998, the New York State Attorney General's office brought civil charges against Casino International, an Antigua-based Internet gaming company, for several violations of state gaming laws. This action was taken pursuant to New York state law forbidding all forms of gambling except the state lottery. The Attorney General's office alleged that Casino International maintained an illegal Internet gaming site in the United States through two Internet Service Providers (ISP) based in Long Island, New York.

The gaming company failed to respond to the state's charges, and in May 1999, a default judgment was issued. According to the Attorney General's office, Casino International distributes its gaming website through ISPs in every U.S. state. Although the company claims to be licensed by the Antiguan government, the Free Trade Zone Commission, which is the official licensing body, does not support this claim.

According to the Attorney General's office, the settlement did not hold the New York ISPs responsible for the alleged violation. The Attorney General's office likened the ISP's position to that of an express mail service that unknowingly delivered illegal drugs; as part of the injunctive relief in the case, the New York ISPs were simply forbidden to continue the practice.

New York also brought a civil case in 1998 against World Interactive Gaming Corporation, an Internet casino operator and a subsidiary of Florida-based Atlantic International Entertainment, for fraudulent solicitation of stock investments and for violation of several federal and state gambling laws based on operation of an Internet casino. That case is pending.

Wisconsin

In September 1997, the State of Wisconsin filed suit against three Internet gaming operations: Net Bet, Online International, Inc., and the Coeur d'Alene Indian lottery.

Net Bet, based in Nevada, operated Casinos of the South Pacific in the Cook Islands, whose website advertisement said that only residents of Nevada, Minnesota, New Jersey, and the Cook Islands were prohibited from placing legal bets. In May 1998, the Net Bet defendants agreed to include Wisconsin in their list of prohibiting jurisdictions and to cease sending betting information into Wisconsin.

Online International, Inc., a Wisconsin-based corporation, planned to operate an Internet gaming website from a location in that state to supply Internet gaming to jurisdictions outside the United States. In late 1998, the corporation was ordered by the court to dissolve. In the third case, that of the Coeur d'Alene Indian lottery, the court held that the tribe was immune from suit but that Wisconsin does have jurisdiction over Unistar, the company engaged by the tribe to run its Internet lottery. Unistar was alleged to have advertised gaming on a website aimed at Wisconsin residents (an action that the tribe could not authorize outside its reservation), misrepresenting the legality of gambling in the state. In May 1999, after the tribe and Unistar had shut down their lottery following a separate court ruling in Idaho, they agreed not to offer the lottery to Wisconsin residents until they had obtained a specific ruling on its legality from a court in Wisconsin.

PRIVATE LAWSUITS

Private lawsuits also have set precedents for the nature and treatment of Internet gaming. In 1997 a Texas citizen, Tom Thompson, sued Handa-Lopez, Inc., operator of the Curaçao-licensed Casino Royale Internet casino, for nonpayment of winnings. In a case before the United States District Court, Western District of Texas, the company claimed it had aimed no explicit advertising at Texas, and hence had established none of the contacts that are necessary for a state to have jurisdiction. The plaintiff argued (and the court agreed) that the act of Internet advertising implicitly includes everyone in the world able to access the website, thus automatically establishing the minimum contact that is needed for due process. Here the court confirmed what some Internet gaming enterprises say is a fundamental principal: if they seek business worldwide, they must be prepared to operate lawfully worldwide.

In 1998 a different type of court test challenged the status quo of Internet gaming operations. After losing more than $70,000 in gambling on at least ten different Internet sites, California resident Cynthia Haines was sued by her bank for nonpayment of the accrued debt on several credit cards. Haines countersued, claiming that the credit card companies were profiting from Internet gaming activity, and argued that such profit taking is both illegal and unfair because no authority regulates Internet gaming. The defendants argued that the case was inadequate because the plaintiff had sued only the credit card companies and not the Internet gaming companies, and that in California such a case could not be based on admittedly illegal conduct by the plaintiff. Experts projected that a finding for the plaintiff could end the credit-card option for Internet gaming companies, forcing them to rely on other forms of payment. Beginning in July 1999, a series of out-of-court settlements were reached with the companies that Haines had sued.

As a result of the Haines case, MasterCard has announced rules for the use of its credit cards for Internet gambling. According to the new rules, in the future all Internet casino merchants seeking to use MasterCard must post on their websites a notice that Internet gaming may not be legal in the state where a potential participant is located, and that it is the responsibility of the consumer to ascertain his/her state's legal position. In addition, Internet merchants must ascertain and record the state or country of each potential customer, and card-issuing institutions such as banks must receive notice of all Internet gaming transactions. Such notification make it possible to code records for future reference. According to MasterCard, the new rules are an effort to accommodate the wide variations in the legal status of Internet gaming around the world and the role of MasterCard as a payment system for individuals, banks, and merchants in many different countries. Visa International has adopted similar requirements for its merchants. (See Appendix G for a discussion of Internet gaming regulation around the world.)

THE INTERACTIVE GAMING COUNCIL

In 1996, Internet gaming companies formed the Interactive Gaming Council (IGC), an international trade group within the Interactive Services Association (ISA). The stated goals of the IGC are to provide a forum for legitimate companies to discuss problems and advance their interests, to establish fair industry guidelines that will improve customer confidence, and to represent the industry in public policy discussions and disseminate information about such issues. The IGC now has at least 55 members, but only a partial membership list is available because some companies prefer not to be publicly identified.

The Council has pushed for an industry-wide code of conduct that would include, inter alia, truth in advertising, privacy and confidentiality for customers, strict licensing requirements, and observance of the gaming laws of jurisdictions from which customers may be placing bets. In 1998 the IGC proposed

an independent, international Internet Gaming Control Board that would be overseen by the ISA and would establish an international certification and regulation system for Internet gaming licensees.

CONCLUSION

Two diametrically opposed regulatory philosophies currently exist with regard to Internet gaming: a strategy calling for legalization and regulatory controls and a strategy prohibiting such activity. Opposition in the United States to legalized Internet gaming is based on several factors. First, there is the fear that Internet gaming and, more specifically, the underlying financial activity, offer unique opportunities for money laundering, fraud, and other crimes. Government officials have also expressed concerns about underage gaming and addictive gambling, which some claim will increase with the spread of Internet gaming. Others point to the fact that specific types of Internet gaming may already be illegal under state laws.

On the other side of the argument is the strategy of legalization and regulation, which is urged by the IGC on behalf of the worldwide industry. Many countries subscribe to this approach and have found that strategies other than prohibition are workable from their own economic and law-enforcement perspectives.

Regardless of which strategy is pursued, technological advances are likely to have great impact on the development and implementation of policy. For example, in 1998, Atlantic International Entertainment announced plans to develop a "portable gaming center" that would bring virtual casinos and sports betting to conventional television sets via telephone lines. Such a device would make offshore gaming operations available to customers who do not have computers or Internet access.

Technology is also moving the industry rapidly toward a point where financial transactions can be fully opaque. Although electronic cash has not "arrived" in the commercial world at large, it is being mentioned with increasing frequency by Internet gaming sites as a way to guarantee security, a factor which experts cite as one of the chief concerns of potential Internet gaming customers.

APPENDICES

APPENDIX A

SMART CARD TECHNOLOGY AND SECURITY

TECHNOLOGY

Multi-application Operating Systems and Interoperability

Cards that contain chips capable of performing multiple tasks are regarded as the future of the smart card industry. Despite the fact that e-cash has proven successful as a stand-alone in Europe, it is not enough simply to offer stored value. This point was made in two pilot programs in the United States, one with VisaCash at the 1996 Summer Olympic Games in Atlanta, Georgia, the other involving VisaCash and Mondex in 1997-98 in New York City, New York. The results were disappointing, according to industry executives. Usage was low, technical glitches hindered transactions in New York, and both trials showed that unless the smart card offered other applications in addition to stored value, American consumers saw no advantages in using it as opposed to cash, debit, or credit cards. Consequently, major smart card systems are developing and perfecting cards that combine e-cash functions with such tasks as building access, personal computer access, and participation in retail loyalty programs.

Combining functions on one card presents problems, however. For example, 'firewalls' need to be constructed between different applications so that one application does not interfere with another. Many industry analysts also caution against expecting that a single 'supercard' can do everything, everywhere; they say that it might make better sense for a card to house logically connected functions.

In such a scenario, a consumer might carry one card housing personal information such as medical and insurance data; another card for business authentication, including building access and travel; and yet a third card with a series of e-purse applications for cash replacement. From a business perspective, in instances where multiple applications reside on a single card, the companies involved in the shared project will have to work out which company owns what aspect of any given project and how it is to be managed.

Both MasterCard and Visa are currently promoting their respective operating systems as the best standard for multi-application cards. MasterCard has developed and is testing a multi-application operating system called MULTOS; the system is based on Mondex technology and can be openly licensed. To promote MULTOS, MasterCard created an industry consortium in 1997 called MAOSCO (Multi-Application Operating System Company) that includes American Express, Europay International, and Mondex International. Visa has countered with the Visa Open Platform, Visa's version of a Java Card that uses the Java software language. MULTOS and the Visa Open Platform offer a path away from the proprietary systems that have characterized the smart card industry to date.

In October 1998, Microsoft Corporation announced that it was developing a smart card operating system for use with its Windows software. Microsoft released the new system, called Windows for Smart Cards, in mid-November 1999. Company executives said that the first application of the card would be in the mobile phone market, but they foresaw network access, loyalty, health care, debit and credit, and cash applications in the future. At the end of 1999, at least 30 trials and projects were reported underway in Europe and North America using Windows for Smart Cards.

The quest for multi-application cards makes interoperability among different systems essential. Currently there are about 20 different systems. Interoperability involves creating industry standards that allow different ware developers to easily join a given operating system and coordinating different organizations in order to complete a common transaction. Some analysts say that designing a common operating system, that is, getting cards from different issuing organizations to work in each other's readers, is less the issue than is the development of a common set of specifications governing the behavior of specific functions (such as debiting, crediting, or e-purse transactions).[26]

With respect to e-purse applications and interoperability, MasterCard stands behind its Mondex e-purse scheme. In March 1999, Visa, American Express, and Europay International countered with the release of what they called Common Electronic Purse Specifications (CEPS). CEPS is intended to define the requirements for all components needed to implement a globally interoperable electronic purse system. Visa claims that organizations representing more than 90 percent of the world's electronic purse cards have agreed to implement CEPS. Visa intends to use the Proton World International consortium, which Visa joined in mid-1998, to support CEPS. In mid-November 1999, Proton World demonstrated the first e-purse based on CEPS technology, the first step in what the consortium hopes will be a full-scale rollout of CEPS-enabled smart cards by 2001.

Chips

Most current research on smart card technology is focusing on improvements in chip capacity, card packaging, and readers. Smart cards may be grouped into three basic chip types: serial memory, protected memory, and microprocessor. Serial memory cards offer no protection or security. Protected memory cards are the most frequently used smart card and are typically used to store units, tokens, or monetary value. The most secure smart card is the microprocessor card. The semiconductor industry continues to introduce new smart card chips that have more processing power and memory than older versions, allowing chips to store more sophisticated operating systems and encryption data.

Card Packaging

Advances are also being made in the areas of card packaging and readers. The vast majority of smart cards in circulation today are "contact" smart cards. When such a card is being used, the gold contact plate on the card must make physical contact with a reader in order for information to be read from the chip. "Contact" smart cards with a magnetic stripe are called hybrids (see Smart Cards).

Card Readers

In addition to developing a new generation of chips and contactless cards, terminal manufacturers are delivering a wide variety of smart card readers, including telephone readers. Some leading manufacturers, for example, are shipping computer keyboards with built-in card readers. Most of the major point-of-sale manufacturers, including Verifone and Hypercom, have released a new generation of point-of-service terminals, all smart card enabled. New classes of devices—network computers, for example—feature integrated smart card readers.

SECURITY

Smart cards have been touted as intrinsically secure devices. If proper security and authentication measures have been built into them, smart cards are arguably more secure than cash, simple debit cards, or magnetic stripe cards. They are considered safe places to store valuable information such as account numbers, passwords, personal information such as medical records, and monetary value. In the case of multi-application cards, before any of the card's applications such as e-purse can be activated, an identity for that application must be established either by the cardholder or by the terminal into which the card is inserted. When the application runs, it can only access data and perform operations that have been explicitly allocated to the established identity.

Security is not an issue for some types of stored-value cards. Disposable cards, for example, available from card dispensing machines, are not specific to the card holder. Merely a convenient substitute for cash, they do not require authentication; their stored value is available to whoever happens to hold the card. Many smart cards, however, especially those featuring electronic purses, often require some form of user identification or authentication as protection against unauthorized access. This type of security not only protects the card purchaser's "stored value," but also the card issuer's investment; the latter may lose money if the value in the electronic purse can be manipulated or counterfeited.

Current means of securing stored-value smart cards include passwords or personal identification numbers (PINs), and physical or behavioral characteristic (biometric) checks.[27] Each system has its advantages and disadvantages. Although passwords allow

the user to delegate the authority to use them, they can be learned by subterfuge, guessed, or given away. In addition, physical and behavioral characteristics can vary or even change outright; they are also often difficult to transmit via telephone lines. These identification methods may be used independently, or, alternatively, in combination; for example, identification may require a card and password or card and biometric.

PINS

The most common form of personal identification is the password or PIN. A PIN's biggest advantage is its low cost. Because the PIN is either right or wrong, the software required to check the PIN is quite simple. PINs are well suited to situations in which the value to be protected is small, such as is the case with e-purses. They are not well suited to high-security applications because of the reasons cited above.

Better security results when passwords are combined with another form of identification. An example of the latter form of authentication is a new, lightweight smart card reader for personal computers. The card reader allows a user to enter a PIN on a PC keyboard, where it is validated by a smart card. However, the validation occurs without PC processing, which might result in a breach of security.

Digital Signatures

Signature verification, or digital signature, is an increasingly popular form of user identification. One of its greatest advantages is portability. Smart cards using such a verification system allow a user to carry a digital signature from one PC to another and enable the user to conduct secure electronic transactions from any computer.

Biometrics

So-called biometric methods of authentication encompass finger/thumbprint, hand geometry, eye scans (retina and iris), and even facial recognition.[28] Different biometrics use different body characteristics, but the principle is fundamentally the same in all cases. Using a camera, sensor, or other device, a person's physical trait is digitized, encrypted, and filed away in a database.

Finger/thumbprint is the oldest form of remote identification test and relies upon systems that can capture the minutiae of a fingerprint. Depending on the system, resolution can be quite coarse. Retina scanning has been used for several years. It has mostly yielded to the newer technique of iris scanning, however, which appears to be the more reliable of the two optical scanning approaches. Such scanning measures the flecks in the iris of the eye, which have been found to be stable over time.

Biometrics offer great advantages in authenticating identity, especially if they are used in conjunction with a PIN or another identification method. They and other authentication methods are part of a larger concern with security vis-à-vis stored-value smart cards. The industry is constantly searching for new and better techniques to protect stored-value cards, especially their chips. Although the chips on cards themselves are generally secure, they can potentially leak information during a transaction with a reader. To foil potential hackers, chip makers have been searching for both software and hardware improvements. Among the techniques being considered is the insertion of digital "noise" into the transaction to mask voltage switching patterns in the chip. Such "noise" does not affect the performance of the card but does make it more difficult for hackers to pinpoint patterns in the chip's operations.[29]

Finally, all types of smart cards operate as part of a larger security system that includes terminals, readers, and personal computers. As industry spokesmen point out, any security chain is only as strong as its weakest link. This maxim is definitely the case with smart card systems. Breaches can occur at any point along the security chain, not just in the card itself. In many cases, these spokesmen say, there may be easier ways to obtain information or financial value than by compromising a smart card.

APPENDIX B

INTERNATIONAL REGULATION OF ELECTRONIC CASH

EUROPEAN REGULATION

In contrast with the United States, European nations have been engaged— at least nominally— in the regulation of electronic cash in its smart card guise. In July 1998, the European Commission, a body that proposes legislation for the European Community, issued new proposed regulatory directives for the use of electronic cash that were designed to "facilitate the development of electronic commerce within the EU "and to "[create] legal certainty for electronic money. "³⁰ The directives seek to establish a regulatory framework in which minimum rules would strengthen confidence in electronic cash by businesses and consumers. According to these minimum rules, consumers would be permitted to use electronic cash to make small payments in euros, the new European currency in limited use as of January 1999, without having to convert national currencies; traditional credit institutions and other firms issuing electronic cash would be regarded as equal financial entities; and electronic cash institutions would be able to offer services throughout the EU provided they were under the supervision of their home countries.

The first of two proposed directives would modify the definition of credit institutions to include electronic cash firms. Such firms would be permitted to operate throughout the EU even if they did not offer a full range of banking services. They would, however, be subject to EU banking regulations, including reserve requirements.

The second directive would restrict the business activities of electronic cash institutions to the issuance of electronic cash and closely related financial and non-financial services, as yet undefined. It would also require them to abide by a set of rules, including authorization by competent authorities; minimum initial capitalization of ECU 500,000 (US$550,000); restriction of investments to liquid, low-risk assets; sound management practices; and adherence to prior EU money laundering and supervision directives. The proposed directives have been submitted to the EU's Council of Ministers and the European Parliament for adoption. If accepted, they would be legally binding on all 15 states.

The European Commission regards its proposed directives as a model framework not just for Europe but for the entire world. At a forum in Washington, D.C., in early December 1998, the Commission's Director-General told his U.S. audience that Europeans regard the directives as entirely compatible with a global approach because they are limited, consumer-friendly, and flexible. He noted Europe's natural advantages in dealing with electronic cash and commerce across national borders, given that Europeans live in an environment where cross-border activity is already a reality.

Financial Action Task Force

To facilitate cooperation on the international level, the Financial Action Task Force (FATF) was created in 1989 by the Group of Seven (G-7) Heads of State to combat global financial crime. FATF currently consists of 26 countries plus the European Commission and the Gulf Cooperation Council. Its membership includes the major financial center countries of Europe, North America, and Asia. Its goal

---

is the development and promotion of policies to combat money laundering, specifically requesting that its members adopt and implement legal, financial, and law-enforcement anti-money laundering standards.

FATF has discussed regulation of electronic cash as part of the larger issue of money laundering on national and international levels. Consequently, provisions governing electronic cash are often grouped with other financial controls pertaining to money laundering and even to electronic commerce via the Internet.

Basic to FATF's work are "The Forty Recommendations of the Financial Action Task Force on Money Laundering," drafted in 1990 and revised in 1996.[31] These recommendations set out a basic framework for anti-money-laundering efforts covering the criminal justice system and law enforcement, the financial system and its regulation, and international cooperation. All nations, not just FATF members, were encouraged to adopt the recommendations. By late 1998, all FATF members had enacted some form of anti-money-laundering legislation in accordance with FATF's basic directives.

Although the recommendations mostly address financial regulatory and law enforcement controls, one recommendation alerted member states to "pay special attention to money-laundering threats inherent in new or developing technologies that might favor anonymity," referring to developing electronic means of payment. This concern with new payment methods figured prominently in two FATF reports, "FATF-IX Report on Money Laundering Typologies "(February 1998) and "FATF-X Report on Money Laundering Typologies " (February 1999).[32] Both reports expressed concern about the potential use by money launderers of stored-value smart cards, online banking, and electronic cash payments in so far as they involve rapidity and anonymity of transactions, broken or missing audit trails, and independence of the traditional banking system. Recommendations included placing limits on the functions and capacity of stored-value smart cards, including maximum value and turnover limits; linking the new technologies to financial institutions and bank accounts; and standardizing record-keeping by financial institutions.

FATF experts noted in their 1999 report that in the absence of specific national legislation, decisions to add these recommendations to electronic payment systems had so far been left to system developers. They warned that without consistent standards and appropriate regulatory oversight, the new payment technologies would undoubtedly prove attractive to money launderers. At the same time, they reported that there were no known instances of money laundering involving the new technologies.

APPENDIX C

LEADING U.S. INTERNET BANKS

The following are among the top-ranked Internet banks cited by Gomez Advisors as of late 1999:

- Security First Network Bank <http://www.sfnb.com> was the first United States bank to offer fully transactional electronic-banking services over the Internet. The bank was granted Office of Thrift Supervision (OTS) approval on May 10, 1995, and opened to the public on October 18, 1995.[33] The bank's website offered what it calls "some pretty compelling reasons "for banking with it. For example, for the first six months, the bank charged no monthly maintenance fees and no required minimum balance. After the trial period, the account remained free so long as the customer maintained a minimum balance of $1,000 or made a monthly direct deposit. The bank also offered its customers 20 free electronic payments monthly and a free ATM or debit card, as well as a free first order of paper checks. The bank promoted "some of the highest "Money Market and CD rates (unspecified) with protection by "military grade "security, FDIC insurance, and its own no-risk guarantee. In 1998 Security First sold its banking operations to the Royal Bank of Canada and announced it would concentrate on selling its Internet banking technology through its subsidiary, Security First Technologies (S1).

- Netb@nk <http://www.netbank.com>, a thrift institution, was granted OTS approval on July 14, 1997. AIB became the first approved and regulated all-Internet bank and the second OTS-approved Internet institution. Net.B@nk of Roswell, Georgia, is the bank's official title.[34]

- CompuBank <http://www.compubank.com>, headquartered in Houston, Texas, was launched in October 1998. The bank was the first virtual bank granted a national charter from the OCC. It qualifies for FDIC insurance and also offers its customers insurance protection from unauthorized transactions from their accounts.[35] The bank pays a $20 finders fee per depositor for new Internet accounts. The OCC charter allows the bank to perform transactions on a nationwide basis. CompuBank is also a member of the Federal Reserve Bank system.

- In November 1998, Wells Fargo Bank <http://www.wellsfargo.com> announced new online banking initiatives. Two pilot locations— each with five computer terminals with Internet connections— were set up on the campuses of the University of Washington in Seattle, and the University of Nevada, Las Vegas. (Each site also has two employees on hand to answer customer questions.) College campuses were chosen because bank officials believed that students would be more open to using online banking options than most bank customers. To attract student accounts, the branches initiated extended hours, from 7:00 a.m. to 7:00 p.m.[36]

- USAccess Bank <http://www.usaccess.bank.com>, a branchless Internet bank, began operations on February 1, 1999, claiming to be the first Internet bank to provide direct Internet lending.[37] The bank, a division of Central Bank USA Inc., part of the holding company structure of Porter Bancorp, offers the usual online banking services, but distinguishes itself from its competitors because it "grants same-day loan approvals— secured and unsecured— as well as lines of credit over the Internet."

- The First Internet Bank of Indiana <http://www.firstib.com> began operations on February 22, 1999. Chartered by the state's Department of Financial Institutions on October 9, 1997, and approved by the FDIC on October 27, 1998, the bank's founders say it is the first state-chartered virtual bank. The bank offers checking, money market savings, CDs, loans, credit cards, and ATM cash cards, with services provided through Virtual Financial Services Inc.'s FiNet front-end software.[38] In the future, the bank plans to offer online images of cleared checks, electronic delivery of periodic account statements, and mortgage loans.

- TeleBank <http://www.telebank.com>, a branchless Internet-based bank located in Arlington, Virginia, that is insured by the FDIC, offers a variety of Internet banking deposit products, including CDs and interest checking, and money market and savings accounts. As of March 1999, TeleBank did not originate loans, but did seek to purchase secured mortgages. Because of TeleBank's deal with Yahoo Finance, customers who open accounts through that portal are required to maintain a balance of $1,000 to qualify for ATM refunds. The program, ATM Refunder, seeks to win customers by automatically refunding ATM fees— up to $6 per month— imposed by other banks on customer accounts.[39] In January 1999, TeleBank became the first virtual bank to cross the $2 billion deposit threshold, the first such bank to be counted among the top 50 federally chartered savings banks.[40] In June 1999, Telebanc Financial Corporation, the parent company of TeleBank, and

E*Trade Group, Inc. announced that they would merge. The merger, approved in January 2000, unites the nation's largest "pure-play Internet bank" with an online personal financial services company. In January 1999, E*Trade Group, Inc. announced that it would bring investment banking services to the Internet in a new company called E*Offering.

- Chase Manhattan Bank <http://www.chase.com> officially inaugurated Internet banking in February 1999— for free. Chase Online Banking will deliver real-time account data to consumers and small-business customers. Chase has enrolled 400,000 online customers since 1997 and is still adding 1,000 daily.[41]

- Salem Five Cents Savings <http://www.salemfive.com>, a small private bank in Salem, Massachusetts, is one of the nation's top Internet banks. The first bank to go online in New England, and one of the first nationwide, Salem Five has $1 billion in assets, with more than $60 million in virtual bank deposits. Chairman and Chief Executive Officer William Mitchelson says that Internet deposits lag behind other delivery channels, but are growing exponentially as the younger customer base becomes more affluent and more computer literate. Mitchelson sees retaining traditional customers as the new challenge inasmuch as Internet banking provides opportunities for consumers to bank anywhere.[42]

- Bank of America's interactive division <http://www.bankamerica.com> plans to offer its online banking customers simple account activity on PalmPilot. (Services are offered on PalmVII; testing began in 1999.[43]) This service is another example of banks having to offer unique services to attract customers.

APPENDIX D

A SAMPLE OF INTERNATIONAL INTERNET BANKS AND WEBSITES, FEBRUARY 2000

[This is by no means an exhaustive list.]

ASIA AND PACIFIC

Australia

Advance Bank	http://www.stgeorge.com.au
BankSA	http://www.banksa.com.au
Suncorp Metway	http://www.suncorpmetway.com.au
Westpac	http://www.westpac.com.au
[includes ChallengeBank and Bank of Melbourne customers]	

Hong Kong

Chekiang First Bank	http://www.cfb.com.hk/cfb/english/intro.html

Malaysia

Southern Berhad Bank	http://www.sbbgroup.com.my

New Zealand

BankDirect [ASB Bank Limited]	http://www.bankdirect.co.nz
National Bank of New Zealand	http://www.nationalbank.co.nz

Thailand

Thai Farmers Bank	http://www.tfb.co.th

CENTRAL AND SOUTH AMERICA/CARIBBEAN

Argentina

Banco Francés	http://hb.bbv.com.ar

Brazil

Banco Boavista [BoavistaNet]	http://boavista.com.br
Banco Itaú	http://www.itau.com.br
Banco do Estado de Sao Paulo [Banespa]	http://www.banespa.com.br
Bradesco [BradescoNet]	http://www.bradesco.com.br

Chile

Banco Santiago	http://www.bsantiago.cl

Colombia

Sucursal Virtual Bancolombia	http://www.bancolombia.com.co

Ecuador

Filanbanco	http://www.filanbanco.com/es

Guatemala

Multibanco	http://www.bancafe.com.gt

Mexico

Grupo Financiero Bital	http://www.bital.com.mx

Paraguay

Interbanco	http://www.infonet.com.py/interbanco
Banco Real	http://www.bancoreal.com.py

Peru

Banco Wiese Sudomeris	http://www.wiese.com.pe

NORTH AMERICA

Canada

Bank of Montreal	http://www.bmo.com
Toronto Dominion Bank	http://www.tdaccess.com

EUROPE

Austria

Bank Austria   http://www.bankaustria.com
P.S.K. Telebanking   http://www.psk.co.at
Steiermärkische Bank und Sparkassen
                                            http://www.bank-styria.co.at

Belgium

KBC Banque & Assurance   http://www.kbc.be

Finland

Merita   http://www.merita.fi

France

Banque Directe   http://www.Banquedirecte.fr
BNP   http://www.bnpgroup.com
Crédit Agricole   http://www.credit-agricole.fr
Crédit Lyonnais   http://www.creditlyonnais.com
Crédit Mutuel   http://www.creditmutuel.fr

Germany

Dresdner Bank   http://www.dresdner-bank.de
National Bank   http://www.nationalbank.de
Raiffeisen-Volksbank eG Mainz   http://www.rvb.de
Stadtsparkasse Köln   http://www.stadtsparkasse.de

Ireland

AIB   http://www.24hour-online.ie

Italy

Banca di Roma   http://www.bancaroma.it
Banca Popolare Commercio
       e Industria   http://www.bpci.it
Banca Popolare di Milano   http://www.bpm.it

Latvia

Paritate Bank   http://www.paritate.com

Sweden

S-E-Banken   http://www.swp4.vv.sebank.se
FörenginsSparbanken   http://www.foreningssparbanken.se
Postbanken   http://www.postbanken.se
Handelsbanken   http://www.handelsbanken.se

Switzerland

Banque Cantonale Vaudoise   http://www.bcv.ch
Basler Kontonalbank   http://www.bkb.ch
Crédit-Suisse   http://www.en.credit-suisse.ch/directnet
BEKB/BCBE   http://www.bekbnet.ch
Solothurner Bank SoBa   http://www.soba.ch
UBS   http://www.ubs.com

United Kingdom

Barclays Bank   http://www.is.barclays.co.uk
Bristol & West   http://www.bristol-west.co.uk/
Nationwide Building Society   http://www.nationwide.co.uk

AFRICA AND MIDDLE EAST

Israel

Israel General Bank   http://www.igb.co/il

Jordan

Arab Bank in Jordan   http://www.bankarabi.com

Nigeria

First City Merchant Bank   http://www.fcmb-ltd.com/fcmb_ebanking.htm
Allstates Trust Bank   http://www.allstates.com.ng/service.htm

South Africa

Nedbank   http://www.nedbank.co.za
First National Bank   http://www.fnb.co.za

APPENDIX E

ELECTRONIC BANKING AROUND THE WORLD

Electronic banking has taken hold across the United States and is extending its reach into other geographic areas of the world, especially those where infrastructure and demographics are in place to support such communications. Although electronic banking is more widespread in parts of Europe, Central and South America, and Asia than it is in Africa and the Middle East, it is difficult to pinpoint geographic concentrations. In many cases, the structure and language of promotional materials make it difficult to ascertain whether a particular institution offers telephone, electronic, PC banking, or Internet banking—the latter with actual transactional capabilities—or whether the website merely offers an interactive or informational service. In general, experience with virtual banks outside the United States has been limited to online brokerage firms and Internet divisions of traditional financial institutions.

The paragraphs that follow are intended solely to provide a frame of reference for understanding how electronic banking activities are developing worldwide.

The number of overseas institutions offering electronic banking services continues to increase. Some of the growth in this area comes from banks that already have a large international and domestic presence. For example, Citibank, which has a worldwide network, offers Internet banking, but only in some of the countries in which it has branches, such as Belgium, Brazil, Germany, Hong Kong, and the United Kingdom. Citibank s PC banking activities, however, are much more widespread.

There are numerous links to international banking sites on the World Wide Web; however, close examination reveals that although a number of sites provide some degree of transactional capability, others are posted exclusively for advertising purposes. In this report, attempts were made to be as thorough as possible and to differentiate between the two types of sites. Examples of non-U.S. banks offering electronic banking services follow.

Caribbean/Central America/South America

Electronic banking, particularly Internet banking, is not yet widespread in the Caribbean/Central America/South America region. Branches of large international banks, for example, Citibank and ABN AMRO, are more likely to have transactional websites than are indigenous banks. One notable exception is Bank Bital, a Mexican bank that offers full service Internet banking. Several Brazilian banks also offer electronic banking services, including Banco Boavista and Banco Itaú. Other banks in South America with transactional capabilities include: Banco Francés < http://hb.bbv.com.ar > (with branches in Argentina, Uruguay, Brazil, and the Cayman Islands); Paraguay s Interbanco < http://www.infonet.com.py/interbanco > and Banco Real < http://www.bancoreal.com.py >; Peru s Banco Wiese Sudameris < http://www.wiese.com.pe >.

Western Europe

Electronic banking services generally are available throughout Western Europe. According to Forrester Research Inc., Europe s move to Internet banking services—mostly in the form of traditional banking operations—will be led by Germany and Switzerland.[44] This forecast is supported by Deutsche Bank's February 1999 announcement that it plans to merge Bank 24, a bank conducting business both telephonically and over the Internet, with its 1,450 retail branches. The new bank, called Deutsche Bank 24, combines branch and direct banking into a single entity.[45]

A variety of other German banks offer electronic banking services: National-Bank <http://www.nationalbank.de>, Dresdner Bank <http://www.dresdner-bank.de>, and Stadtsparkasse Köln <http://www.stadtsparkasse.de>.

Numerous Swiss banks offer electronic banking services: BEKB/BCBE <http://www.bekbnet.ch>, Solothurner Bank SoBa <http://www.soba.ch>, Banque Cantonale Vaudoise <http://www.bcv.ch>, Basler Kantonalbank <http://www.bkb.ch>, UBS <http://www.ubs.com>, and Credit Suisse <http://www.en.credit-suisse.ch/directnet>. Interestingly, the latter's website contains the following disclaimer: "...the services and securities otherwise offered in these Web Sites are for legal reasons not being offered in the United States, to U.S. residents or U.S. persons as defined under US securities law. The same is true for residents of the UK and Japan. " None of the other Swiss banking sites contains such a notice.

France's Crédit Agricole <http://www.paris.credit-agricole.fr> uses a unique strategy to entice customers to Internet banking: a satellite television connection. The bank's project manager noted that although computer ownership is "fairly low " in France, almost every household has a television set. Hence, Crédit Agricole, working with the French satellite television provider TPS, introduced its own TPS

channel, CA TV, which allows TPS customers to conduct electronic banking activities through their television sets. Bank management reported that if customers accept TPS they will be ready to transition to Internet banking once the capability for satellite connection to the Internet becomes available.[46]

Sweden was one of the first countries to offer Internet banking. In late 1997, it was reported that 11 of Sweden's biggest banks had, or were planning to offer, Internet banking in 1998.[47] In 1998, it was noted that one of the country's largest banks had 100,000 customers with Internet banking accounts. The Postbanken notes on its website <http://www.posten.postnet.se>, however, that a Swedish personal number or Norwegian or EU country citizenship is required for use of its Internet payment service.

Banks in the United Kingdom also offer Internet services. For example, from about mid-October 1998 through the end of the year, Prudential, a life assurance company in the United Kingdom, drew about 150,000 customers with its launch of "Egg, "an Internet banking service offering an eight percent interest rate. As a result of the influx, the company was overwhelmed and had to double its staff to 150 persons.[48]

Another British institution, Barclays Bank <http://www.barclays.co.uk>, offers free unlimited access to the Internet through its Barclays.net service, which enables its customers to sign up for Internet banking services. The Barclays.net service is free to the bank's customers other than for the cost of a local telephone call while online.

Middle East and Africa

Because of under-developed communications infrastructure, Internet banking does not have a large presence in Africa and the Middle East. Nonetheless, some banks offer electronic banking services. Nigeria's First City Merchant Bank <http://www.fcmb-ltd.com/fcmb_ebanking.htm> provides telephonic e-banking. Another Nigerian bank, Allstates Trust Bank <http://www.allstates.com.ng/service.htm> offers unspecified electronic banking services— the description fits an Electronic Smart Card Account. However, the Allstates site also describes a Unified Banking Service, an independent telecommunications system with satellite earthstations and a microwave radio link for providing online services.

South Africa has several banks with transactional websites. NedBank <http://www.nedbank.co.za/1.online/online_netbank.html> provides full-service banking for clients of its Internet banking arm, NetBank. First National Bank <http://www.fnb.co.za> also offers netbanking services. The Arab Bank in Jordan <http://www.bankarabi.com/ask/faq.html> has a website stating that the bank does not allow clients to use the Internet to open an account with any of its 370 Arab Bank branches worldwide, nor does it provide customer account information over the Internet because of concerns about adequate security. The bank notes, "Should this change in the future, we will definitely consider embarking on the Internet for such requirements." However, the Arab Bank's Phonebank service provides access to accounts at any time, via PIN number, for such services as account balances, transactions, statements, and internal funds transfer within local Arab Bank branches.

Israeli banks began providing limited service over the Internet in 1997, when banks received approval to use it to provide account information; 55,000 customers receive such information. In fact, the website for Israel General Bank <http://www.igb.co/il/bankhtml/english/online_banking.html> notes that its customers can access bank services via the Internet, including information on customer accounts, but that transactions are not yet permitted.

In March 1999, Israel's Supervisor of Banks announced that Israeli banks will be allowed to provide Internet banking transactions, pending approval, after examination of the security of their systems. Customers will be permitted to open savings accounts and buy and sell securities but will not be able to transfer funds from one account to another or to pay bills via the Internet because of security risks.[49] The website for Israel General Bank notes that "once the necessary legal steps have been taken, customers will also be able to implement transactions via the Internet."

Asia and Pacific

Electronic commerce is still evolving in Asia and the Pacific. There is conflicting evidence on the development of electronic banking. Some analysts say it is increasing; others say growth is stagnant because of lack of customer confidence. In addition, a great difference exists among the countries of the region in the level of development and infrastructure needed for electronic commerce. Electronic banking services are currently more widely available in Hong Kong than in other areas.

Chekiang First Bank [Hong Kong] <http://www.cfb.com.hk> has a Web Banking Service available to all of its Phone Banking Service users. Services include time deposit instructions, account transfers, Hong Kong dollar account transfer to a third party account with the bank (maximum daily cycle limit HK $10,000), and buying or selling foreign currencies during office hours. The maximum limit per transaction is HK$500,000 or equivalent.

Hong Kong's JETCO Joint Electronic Teller Services is scheduled to provide its 49-member bank network with Internet banking, the first Internet Certification Authority for such services in Hong Kong. The integration project is led by Hewlett-Packard in partnership with CyberTrust, and will provide the banks with digital certification for Internet-based transactions.

Malaysia's Southern Berhad Bank's Direct Access (SBB Direct) <http://www.sbbgroup.com.my> promotes itself as an electronic banking and commercial site, offering "true direct banking." However, the service is actually an intranet dial-up service. (Because Malaysian regulations do not allow financial transactions to be conducted over the Internet, Internet banking services in Malaysia would be illegal.) Financial transactions must be accessed from the bank's intranet dial-up service—with "every phone a branch..."—and branches operational around

the clock. For persons interested in the bank's services, the website provides phone numbers and an email address.[50]

In April 1998, Thai Farmers Bank <http://www.tfb.co.th> announced a move to target corporate customers and launch Thailand's first Internet banking service in the third quarter, 1998. The bank expected that all of its corporate customers would use Internet banking by 2000.[51] In October 1998, however, the bank announced that Internet banking services would not be provided until early 1999. Initially, banking services will involve customer inquiries concerning account balances and statements, and then will expand to online utility service payments. Full Internet banking services for personal accounts are seen in the future. However, the bank intends to survey customer requirements and patterns before increasing services, particularly because Thailand has "little demand...for the use of the Internet for financial transactions at the moment."[52]

APPENDIX F

INTERNATIONAL REGULATION OF ELECTRONIC BANKING

INTERNATIONAL ORGANIZATIONS

Financial Action Task Force

As noted under 'Financial Action Task Force on Money Laundering "in the 'Electronic Cash "section of this report, the organization has expressed concern about the regulation of Internet banking, particularly in areas where banking operations are protected by a high level of secrecy and little or no proof of identity is needed to open accounts. In its February 1998 report on money laundering trends, the FATF discussed the potential implications of emerging payment systems such as electronic money and Internet transactions. The FATF's February 1999 report also addressed 'misuse of the Internet and other new payment technologies for fraud and the transmission of illicit funds. '[53]

Caribbean Financial Action Task Force

The Caribbean Financial Action Task Force (CFATF), is an organization of Caribbean basin states that have agreed to implement common countermeasures to address the problem of money laundering. At its October 1997 meeting, the CFATF Council of Ministers endorsed a plan to develop a program aimed at sensitizing regional governments to the possibilities of money laundering through emerging cyberspace technologies. Thereafter, a May 1998 workshop was held to discuss 'Money Laundering Through Emerging Cyberspace Technology. "The workshop participants included government officials and industry representatives from approximately 25 nations. CFATF also held a spring 1999 electronic banking seminar to expose senior government officials to emerging technologies and assorted regulatory, legal, and law enforcement policy issues.

Offshore Group of Banking Supervisors

The Offshore Group of Banking Supervisors was established in 1980 as a forum for supervisory cooperation between banking supervisors in offshore financial centers.[54] In 'On-site Examination Checklist, "an annex to *The Supervision of Cross Border Banking*, a report prepared by a working group of members of the Offshore Group of Banking Supervisors and the Basle Committee on Banking Supervision, 18 items of regulatory interest are enumerated as issues to be raised during on-site examinations. Although the checklist does not specifically address electronic banking issues, it does ask what requirements banks and banking groups must fulfill in order to become authorized in their jurisdictions; whether there are differences in types of banking licenses issued and conditions imposed; and whether the home supervisory authorities of such entities are allowed to conduct on-site inspections. These issues are a part of an overall regulatory environment related to electronic banking.

APPENDIX G

INTERNET GAMING REGULATORY POLICY AROUND THE WORLD

REGULATORY POLICY AROUND THE WORLD

In the face of a rapid increase in the Internet gaming industry and the likelihood that it will reach new populations of users in the near future, national governments (and, in some cases, state and regional governments as well) have taken a variety of approaches to regulation. Some have dealt with Internet gaming as an unmitigated threat, some as an economic opportunity, and most as a distinctly mixed blessing that brings unprecedented legal complications. Those three views correspond approximately to three types of strategy for dealing with the new industry: prohibition, regulation, and maintenance of the status quo until the nature of the industry and its problems becomes more clear. In few cases has a final strategy or set of regulations been accepted as fully satisfactory; the phenomenon is too recent and its dimensions are too unlike those of other legal issues for most jurisdictions to have fully determined all the ramifications and turned that understanding into policy. Contributing to uncertainty is the unknown dimension of the industry and the actual rate at which it is growing; collection of industry-wide information on those subjects is obstructed because not all enterprises publicize their profits or business transactions.

ASIA/PACIFIC

Australia

Australia has chosen to permit Internet gaming in a strictly regulated environment, at the level of state and territory government. In the last two years, Australia's efforts to develop a workable system of Internet gaming regulations have attracted considerable attention. Sports and casino betting are extremely popular in Australia; according to the Tasmanian Gaming Commission's figures, in 1997 and 1998 combined gambling expenditures were estimated at about $94 billion. At the same time, use of the Internet has become a very popular activity. State and territory governments in Australia have concluded that these trends will mean that many of their citizens will rapidly become customers of whatever Internet gaming is available, regardless of government actions to control the process.

The Australian Commonwealth government does not currently regulate the domestic gambling industry, except under the Financial Transaction Reports Act of 1988, which was passed to prevent money laundering, large-scale tax evasion, and certain other activities of organized crime. That act designates conventional casinos and online gaming providers as "cash dealers" and requires them to identify customers under certain circumstances. The act also requires cash dealers to report specified types of financial transactions and suspicious transactions to the Australian Transaction Reports and Analysis Centre (AUSTRAC).

In 1997, Australia began working on a national set of guidelines for Internet gaming activity. In 1998 the commonwealth government assigned the project of researching the industry and recommending a national strategy to the Productivity Commission, an independent agency that serves as the Australian government's principal review and advisory body on microeconomic policy and regulation. The commission's draft report was issued in July 1999; the final, three-volume report was issued in December 1999, after a round of consultations with government agencies and public hearings.

Like the report of the United States National Gambling Impact Study Commission, the Productivity Commission report addresses Internet gaming as a segment of the overall gambling issue; the impetus for both reports came from public concerns about gambling in general. The final Australian report, however, devoted 67 pages to "Policy for New Technologies," compared with the more nominal treatment of Internet gaming in the NGISC report. Among the key judgments of the Australian report are the following statements: "There are...grounds for regulation of Internet gambling, along the lines of regulations applying to other gambling forms. The Commission considers that there are ways of controlling online gambling sufficiently to exercise such regulations...," and "Managed liberalisation— with tight regulation of licensed sites to ensure integrity and consumer protection— has the potential to meet most concerns, as long as the approach is national." The Productivity Commission's final report is available at the Internet website <www.pc.gov.au/inquiry/gambling/finalreport>.

The Select Committee on Information Technologies of the Australian Senate also is conducting an inquiry into domestic online gambling. The committee is examining the present extent and impact of online gambling; the feasibility of limiting access, especially for minors; the adequacy of current state and territory regulations on online gambling; and the need for national legislation on the subject. The committee issued a report on its findings in March 2000. Following the issuance of the Productivity Commission's final report, the Australian Prime Minister, disturbed by the rapid growth of Internet gambling, directed that a Ministerial Council on Gambling be formed. That council, which would be formed by the chief ministers of all the states and territories, would investigate the feasibility and consequences of banning Internet gambling.

Regulation at the State and Territory Level

In 1998 and 1999, several Australian jurisdictions prepared or adopted legislation legalizing and regulating Internet gaming. Those jurisdictions include Queensland; the Northern Territory; Tasmania; Norfolk Island (a small offshore island with dependency status); the Australian Capital Territory, which includes Canberra; and most recently Victoria. A national regulatory framework (commonly referred to as the National Model), developed by gaming ministers from all the states, has served as a model for legislation in the states of Queensland and Victoria and in the National Capital Territory. The stated purpose of this framework is to minimize the negative impact of gambling originating from overseas or from illegal sources by providing alternative products that are carefully monitored and, in addition, to prohibit illegal domestic operations that would put customers at risk.

Although several states and territories have enacted regulatory legislation, the types of activity covered and the degree of regulation vary somewhat. The Queensland Interactive Gambling (Player Protection) Act went into effect in October 1998. The most comprehensive of the laws currently in effect, the act stipulates the regulatory framework for interactive gaming, provides for the issuance of licenses to approved recipients, allows for taxes to be levied on licensed operations, and provides a full regime of protections for customers and the community in general. The law also provides for cooperation with other Australian jurisdictions that regulate interactive gaming. Queensland is now accepting license applications.

In Tasmania, legislation was passed in 1998 permitting conventional casinos to offer interactive gaming but prohibiting Tasmanian citizens from participating. In December 1999, existing legislation was amended to permit the issuance of licenses to new interactive gaming providers. Tasmania's law continues to prohibit Tasmanian citizens from participating, however. Norfolk Island has reversed a long-held position against gambling by passing laws permitting and regulating conventional and Internet gaming, but it too prohibits its citizens from participation in Internet wagering. As of January 2000, four Internet license applications were under consideration by the Norfolk Island Gaming Authority, and none had yet been granted. The Australian Capital Territory's legislation, also enacted in 1998, appears aimed primarily at customer protection. License issuance began there at the end of 1998. As of January 2000, New South Wales did not yet have legislation. The Northern Territory has allowed and regulated conventional and Internet gaming for several years.

Australian Regulatory Philosophy

The emphasis on protecting the consumer first, which seems to predominate in most of the Australian jurisdictions, means that gaming sites must prove conclusively that they are well-backed financially and intent on providing reliable service. Among consumer protection provisions are the prohibition of participation by minors and the prohibition of extension of credit; mandatory self-exclusion by problem gamblers; protection of customer privacy; submission to audits; mandatory complaint procedures; and the licensing of all directors, executive officers, and major stockholders.

The approach of Australian jurisdictions to taking bets from customers in the United States varies considerably, and little has been said about establishing a formal policy on this matter. In the absence of formal regulations, individual casinos are deciding how to deal with this issue. Sites in Tasmania and Norfolk Island seem to welcome all patrons while prohibiting local participation. On the other hand, the largest individual Internet operation, Centrebet of Darwin, stopped taking bets from customers in the United States in 1998 pending legislation or other policy determinations in the United States.

The Anti-Gaming Movement

Australia also has a counter-movement that advocates prohibiting rather than regulating Internet gaming. The rapid expansion of conventional gambling services has drawn fire from many politicians. In 1998, a senator representing South Australia proposed to the Productivity Commission that Australia prohibit domestic gaming companies from offering their services via the Internet and prohibit foreign Internet gaming operations from making their services available in Australia. The senator, whose position was supported by the prime minister and the national treasurer, argued that children would have too much access to gambling if it were on the Internet, especially considering children's natural attraction to sports. Coming on the heels of the Productivity Commission's final report, which summarized the first comprehensive investigation of the subject, the Prime Minister's immediate call for continued scrutiny of Internet gambling was widely construed as an escalation of the anti-gambling movement. The Prime Minister stressed particularly the scale of problem gambling; the Productivity Commission reported that 290,000 Australians are problem gamblers, whose addiction causes an estimated loss of US$2 billion annually.

EUROPE AND CANADA

Gaming Regulators European Forum

The 1998 meeting of the Gaming Regulators European Forum in Helsinki issued a Position Statement on Gambling on the Internet. It held that each country should be responsible for policy on such activity in its jurisdiction and that other jurisdictions should respect such policies. It called for full regulation of gaming in countries deciding to allow it, with participation restricted to the residents of that country and to individuals in other countries with which reciprocal agreements exist. Control measures also would address gambling addiction, honest gaming procedures, player confidentiality and security, and prevention of money laundering. No punitive measures would be taken against a bettor participating from a jurisdiction prohibiting such activity. The forum suggested that cross-border controls would have to be at the level of the Internet service provider (ISP). Contracts between ISPs and gaming operators might require that the ISP prevent access to addresses in jurisdictions that are legally off-limits. (The practical possibility of placing such responsibility has been much discussed in the United States and elsewhere; it generally has been concluded that ISPs do not have the capability to monitor the nature of every transmission that passes through them.)

United Kingdom

In the United Kingdom, the National Gaming Board regulates about 120 conventional casinos, many of which are considered by industry experts to be among the world's most reputable gaming companies. Some of the best-known British casinos, such as Victor Chandler, William Hill, Ladbrokes, and Blandford Betting, have used their standing in the traditional gaming industry to move into the Internet field. However, the Gaming Board's most overriding policy is that commercial gaming shall occur only on licensed premises and not on other private property. The board has recognized that Internet gaming inherently belongs to the latter category, but it also recognizes the difficulty of enforcing a ban on such activity. One British gambling expert has expressed the opinion that it likely is legal for a British citizen to bet on the Internet if the host is located in another country, especially if that country is in the European Union. British money-laundering regulations, based on European Council guidelines, apply mainly to financial institutions; however, a Code of Practice for casinos sets strict standards for investigation of suspicious transactions.

After delaying consideration of a ban on Internet gambling in 1999 because of the relatively low occurrence of Internet gaming in Great Britain, in early 2000 the Gaming Board began a review of that phase of the industry. A factor in that review was the start of Internet gaming operations by the major companies listed above, many of which have moved their operations to offshore locations such as Gibraltar and Alderney Island, where Great Britain's wagering taxes (ranging from 6.75 to 9 percent) do not apply. The board is expected to make recommendations on Internet gaming policy sometime in the first half of 2000. A new Gambling Review Body, including experts from a variety of fields, was scheduled to begin a comprehensive review of the entire gambling industry in May 2000, with a final report due in mid-2001. That body's purpose is to recommend changes in the Gaming Act of 1968, considered the most important law covering gambling activities.

Other European Countries

Internet gaming operates in at least three other European countries: Germany, Austria, and Liechtenstein. A government-sanctioned Internet lottery in Finland also has been reported. In Germany, Nierfeld's Internet Casino recently became the first such operation in that country. However, because German law does not permit gambling, either Nierfeld's is operating from another venue and claiming to be German, or it is an illegal operation. Liechtenstein's Millions 2000 Internet lottery, an extension of an existing conventional lottery operation, is run directly by the government and dedicates substantial percentages of its revenues to charities. It is the only such operation in the country. Austria's Interwetten, which began operation in 1989 and established a positive reputation as a phone-betting service, opened an online service in 1997 to expand its market beyond Central Europe. Interwetten now claims to have customers worldwide. Austria prohibits transmission of Internet gaming into the country (making an exception for Millions 2000) and has a strict regulatory system for operations based in Austria.

Canada

Canada appears to be going through the same evaluation process as Australia relative to legalizing and regulating Internet gaming. The Canadian government has declared the importance of gaining control over an industry that could be dangerous to consumers and whose products in fact already are available to Canadians without any effective controls at all. As early as 1997, legislation has been proposed in the Canadian Parliament to regulate Internet gaming. According to the sponsors of the bill, current law prohibits setting up a virtual casino or sportsbook on Canadian soil. Although the bill submitted in 1997 received substantial support in Parliament, it was not enacted, and no legislation on the subject had emerged as of early 1999. In 1998 Canada extended its money laundering statute, which was passed before casino gambling became a significant industry, to include private casinos licensed by Canadian provinces.

THE CARIBBEAN

Caribbean Financial Action Task Force

In May 1998, the Caribbean Financial Action Task Force (CFATF) sponsored an exercise entitled "Exploring Money Laundering Through Emerging Cyberspace Technologies: A Caribbean Based Exercise," in Port of Spain, Trinidad. Representatives included senior-level officials from 25 countries, multinational organizations, and the banking and casino industries. Delegates were confronted with a large number of unique policy issues, including those that pertain to Internet gaming. Much of the focus of the exercise concerned the vulnerability of cyberspace-based payment systems, including Internet casinos, to money laundering and other types of financial fraud.

Several interesting perspectives were offered during the exercise. One such perspective was that different countries had reached divergent conclusions about how to conduct investigations of persons and entities seeking to gain a license to operate gaming establishments in CFATF jurisdictions. In the cyberspace context, licensing was seen as especially critical because of the transborder nature of many of the services delivered through the network. One argument that emerged in the discussions held that jurisdictions with a strong commitment to rigorous and effective oversight of potential Internet gaming establishments could be "held hostage" by the weak enforcement and oversight policies of their neighboring countries. The "cascading downward" effect of regulatory coverage triggered by weak enforcement in any single jurisdiction was argued to be more severe in cyberspace but hardly a unique problem in the region.

The participants also identified the collection of records and other data relating to suspicious financial activities as another important element of any effective system of oversight and supervision. On this issue, it was argued that cyberspace presented a unique series of challenges because the legal status of transaction records was unclear in a number of the jurisdictions represented at the CFATF exercise. Added to this fact was the potential problem of how to share suspicious transaction information across transnational borders. A number of participants noted that evidence obtained in a neighboring jurisdiction would not necessarily be admissible in their courts.

Another subject of considerable comment at the CFATF exercise concerned the role of supervision and external audit in maintaining the integrity of government oversight. On the issue of how to execute "on-site" inspections of Internet gaming establishments, it was broadly acknowledged that new technological means would likely be required in order to establish effective procedures for auditing and analyzing records of these Internet operators. The exercise participants agreed that they should weigh the pros and cons of various regulatory options, including how to address

the types of problems raised above, as they consider Internet casino gaming operations in their jurisdictions.

Antigua

Antigua, which many refer to as the proto-typical Internet gaming base, has the largest concentration of websites among the Caribbean nations. Prior to the expansion of Internet gaming in the mid-1990s, Antigua had no gaming regulatory body and hence no experience in controlling the activities of such an industry. A regulatory structure for Internet gaming has been in place since 1997, when the government passed the "Standard Conditions for Licensing of Virtual Casino Wagering and Sports Book Wagering in the Antigua and Barbuda Free Trade and Processing Zone." That regulation enabled the existing Free Trade and Processing Zone Commission to license approved persons to run the sites, as it does for other types of business in the island's tax-free zone. An anti-fraud division exists to investigate customer complaints.

Among the legal restrictions included in the law are the prohibition of sublicensing and license transfer, of submitting false information during the licensing process, of failure to fulfill all commitments to players, and of making false promotional statements. The law also stipulates that software must be tested and that gaming programs must comply with gaming industry standards. The annual license fee is $100,000 for a casino and $75,000 for a sports book; a 20 percent tax is levied on overseas telephone bills. The Commission claims that its mandatory background check has eliminated 300 applicants. The island now is considering revision of its gaming statutes on the model of Queensland's 1998 Interactive Gambling (Player Protection) Act.

Dominica

The Commonwealth of Dominica, located just south of Antigua, has issued perhaps the most official policy statement supporting gaming and other Internet activities as a part of the country's economic welfare. In mid-1998 the government announced its intention to open the first government-operated Internet casino, specifically noting that no jurisdictions, implicitly including the United States, would be forbidden as targets for transmission.

Dominica also grants gaming licenses by contract with individuals; terms of the contract differ as to the number of nationals to be hired and the duration of the contract, as well as the percentage of gross revenues to be paid to the state (usually 5 percent). If that amount comes to less than $25,000 in a given year, the latter amount is paid. The registration fee is $15,000. Licensees agree to independent auditing and are required to report the addition of any third parties to the enterprise. The license includes favorable terms for international communications access; concessions on work permits and equipment import; and tax exemption on income, revenues, and winnings by non-Dominican customers. Licenses are issued by the Ministry of Finance, Industry and Planning. The government processes license applications with the help of the Domini Corporation, which advertises itself as a government-appointed agent that can guarantee swift processing, provide consultation in developing Internet gaming operations, and provide software and hardware. Domini has "associate law offices" in New York, London, Montreal, and Antigua.

Other Caribbean Nations

Gaming regulations in other Caribbean nations such as St. Kitts, Grenada, and the Netherlands Antilles— all of which have between 10 and 25 gaming sites— do not appear to have any comprehensive provisions. The Internet gaming license in St. Kitts is issued by the Ministry of Trade, Industry, Caricom Affairs, Youth, Sports, and Community Affairs. The one-sentence document says that the cabinet has approved the applicant's request to engage in casino games and sports betting using the Internet.

In some Caribbean nations, the licensing procedure is unclear. In Grenada the licensing authority issue was put in question by a dispute between a gaming site operator that claimed to have received exclusive licensing authority from the government and another operator bearing a license ostensibly issued directly by the government. In the Netherlands Antilles, there is an understanding that disputes over the practices of individual gaming establishments will be resolved according to existing laws, but at present there appear to be no regulatory provisions specifically designated to facilitate the resolution of such disputes.

APPENDIX H

A REPRESENTATIVE LISTING OF INTERNET CASINOS AND SPORTSBOOKS AS OF MID-1999

The table that follows is a compilation of approximately 200 Internet gaming operations. [Note: This list was current as of mid-1999. As the industry is in constant flux, the information should not be interpreted as all-inclusive.] The data are taken from websites, online website listings, and other sources. In the "Location" column, both geographical and website location are given—when available. In some cases, a casino or sportbook name has been identified, but a search has not located a website for that name. The absence of a website may mean that the operation is no longer in business, or it may mean that the website for that operation is found under a different name. If there is specific information that the operation is no longer in business, that fact is noted in the "License" column. In some cases, neither the website nor other information provides the geographic location of the operation. In the "License" column, a definite "yes" or "no" indicates that a specific statement on the site's license has been found; a "n.a." means that no information on that status has been found.

The "Comments" column summarizes several types of other information about the operation that may be of interest: legal status, change of location or status, limitations on users stated on the website, connections with other Internet operations, parent companies or software providers, date established, and languages and games offered. In the first three categories, all such information available has been included; information in the other categories is meant to be representative rather than inclusive.

COMPANY	LOCATION	LICENSE?	COMMENTS
AAA Casino	unknown www.aaacasino.com	n.a.[55]	specific note to U.S. citizens: "don't participate if illegal in your state (Arizona, Illinois, Indiana, Minnesota, Missouri, Nevada, Wisconsin)"; specific note about Indiana
ABC Islands	Costa Rica www.abc.com	yes	moved from Netherlands Antilles 1998
Ace in the Hole Online Casino and Sportsbook	Costa Rica [56]	yes	
Aces Casino and Sportsbook	Margarita Island (Venezuela)	yes; Antigua and Venezuela	est. 1998; English, German, Dutch, Spanish, French
Aces Gold Casino	Curaçao www.acesgold.com	n.a.	est. Oct. 1998
Acropolis Casino	Dominican Republic www.acropoliscasinos.com	yes	

COMPANY	LOCATION	LICENSE?	COMMENTS
Action Sports Wagering	St. Martens, V.I. www.actionsportswagering.com	n.a.	
Active Gaming	Curaçao www.activegaming.com	n.a.	blackjack, baccarat, poker
All-Star Sportsbook	Margarita Island (Venezuela) www.allstarsportsbook.com	yes; Venezuela, Antigua	support company EFS Caribbean; also has computers in Antigua, St. Kitts, and Canada; 23 casino games
Allied Sports	Curaçao	out of business as of 1998	
Antigua Casino and Sportsbook	Antigua www.antigua.org	yes	est. 1999; owned by Playstar Corp. (Canada)
Arizona Sportsbook	Mexico	out of business	
Arrowhead Sportsbook and Casino	St. Kitts www.casinolive.com	yes	uses Carib F/X software
Atlantic City Casino	Antigua www.atlanticcitycasino.com	yes	owned by company in Vancouver, B.C.
Atlantic Interbet Casino	Antigua www.atlanticinterbet.com	yes	
Atlantis Casino	Belize www.casino-atlantis.com	n.a.	owned by Atlantis Gaming, Ltd. of Antigua; sold in 1998 by Atlantis Gaming Co. of U.S.
Avalon Casinos	Dominica www.avaloncasinos.com	yes	est. 1996; states "your local laws must permit betting:
Avatar Casino	Bahamas	yes	est. August 1998; owned by Canadian company; chat feature
Bali Casino	Curaçao www.balicasino.com	n.a.	owned by Curaçao company
Best Bet Casino	Dominica (no website found)	n.a.	bingo, lottery, slots, keno, poker
Best Bet Sports	Costa Rica www.bestbetsports.com	yes	also has casino operation; est. 1996

COMPANY	LOCATION	LICENSE?	COMMENTS
Bid Caesar's Sportsbook	Antigua www.bigcaesars.com	yes	also called Carib Sportsbook and Caribbean Sportsbook
Big Daddy Sportsbook	Costa Rica www.bigdaddy.com	yes	est. 1996; only credit card and bank wire payment
Bingo of the Americas	Costa Rica	yes	parent company Cybergames; revenues to Red Cross of the Americas and First Lady's Charities against Cancer and Infantile Diseases
Bookies Café	Curaçao www.bookiescafe.com	n.a.	
Bowman International	Mauritius, Isle of Man www.bowmans.co.uk	yes	long-time U.K. operation; recently entered Internet
Bugsy Online Casino	Antigua www.bugsyonline.com	yes	est. 1997
Canbet	Australia www.canbet.au.com	yes	small operation; est. 1998, Canberra; software from eCom Solutions, Canberra
Carib Sportsbook	Antigua www.caribsports.com	yes	also known as Boss's Casino (q.v.) Caribbean Sportsbook
Caribbean Cyber Casino	Grenada www.ccasino.com	yes	uses MicroGaming Systems software
Caribbean Health and Housing Foundation	Antigua www.onlinelottery.com	yes	est. 1997
Caribbean Island	Dominican Republic www.caribbeanisland.com	yes	est. June 1998; offers e-commerce using credit card
Casanova's	Trinidad (no website found)	n.a.	one of five casinos run by Sunny Group under name Casino Fortune
Casares	Gibraltar www.casares.com	yes	began 1995 as InterKeno, expanded 1996 ad Bet4ABetterWorld, renamed 1998; 20% of revenues to New World Foundation and other charities
Casino Alitalia	Dominican Republic www.casinoalitalia.com	yes	est. 1998; offers e-commerce with credit cards
Casino Australia	Curaçao www.casinoaustralia.com	n.a.	uses CryptoLogic e-cash; owned by Bardanac Holdings of Netherlands Antilles; "no gambling for money by U.S. players"

COMPANY	LOCATION	LICENSE?	COMMENTS
Casino Café Casino	Netherlands Antilles www.casinocafe.com	n.a.	uses Cyberbookies of North America software; also known as Bookies Casino Café and Sportsbook
Casino Caribe	Dominican Republic www.casinocaribe.com	yes	Japanese and English; market list claims U.S. customers
Casino Cash	Margarita Island www.casinocash.net	yes	
Casino Casino	Dominica (possible) www.casinocasino.com	n.a.	site offers software, turnkey gaming operations, even licenses
Casino CoCo	Costa Rica www.casinococo.com	yes	
Casino-Crystal	Antigua www.casinocrystal.com	n.a.	connected with CasinoInn; uses CryptoLogic e-cash
Casino Fantasy	location unknown www.casinofantasy.com	n.a.	Japanese, English, Chinese, German, Spanish, French; equipment from Cyber Technologies, Inc. of Las Vegas; uses e-cash; site not available to U.S. customers
Casino Fortune	Trinidad www.casinofortune.com	yes	umbrella organization for five casinos (four in Trinidad, one in Botswana); est. January 1997; electronic funds transfer
Casino Forum	Trinidad www.casinoforum.com	n.a.	
CasinoInn	Antigua www.casinoinn.com	yes	branch of World-Wide Telesports (WWTS); uses CryptoLogic e-cash
Casino International	Antigua www.4casino.com	no	has been listed as defunct; branch of WWTS
Casino Internationale	Curaçao www.casino-internationale.com	n.a.	e-cash offered
Casino of the Americas	St. Kitts	out of business	
Casino of the Kings	Antigua www.i-casino.com	n.a.	uses EFS Caribbean equipment; also a sportsbook
Casino on Air	location unknown www.casinoonair.com	no	uses EFS Caribbean software; eight languages

COMPANY	LOCATION	LICENSE?	COMMENTS
Casino-on-Net	Antigua www.casino-on-net.com	n.a.	est. 1997
Casino Regal	location unknown www.casinoregal.com	n.a.	uses CryptoLogic e-cash
Casino Royale	Curaçao www.funscape.com	yes	est. 1995, under Funscape International
Casino Royal Magic	Ireland www.aroyalmagicstreet.com	yes; Ecuador	uses MonaCard encryption system (Monaco) for payment security; administered by Gertman S.A. of Luxembourg
Casino Tokyo	Antigua www.casinotokyo.com	yes	Japanese version of CasinoInn
Casino Tropicale	Costa Rica www.casinotropicale.com	yes	at Hotel Barcelo, Guanacaste; licensed six years for conventional operations
Casino Vega Internet Casino	Costa Rica www.casinovega.com	yes	est. 1999
Casinos of the South Pacific	Cook Islands sp.cosp.com	yes	claimed huge profit first week open
Casinos of the World	St. Kitts www.casinosoftheworld.com	yes	
Centrebet	Brisbane, Australia www.centrebet.com.au	yes	taken over by Jupiters, a large conventional casino, 1998; no U.S. customers served
Classic Casino and Sportsbook	British Virgin Islands www.classiccasino.com	n.a.	eight languages; EFS Caribbean e-cash; owned by SoftecSystems, Vancouver
Club Casino	Liberia (no website found)	n.a.	seven languages; est. 11/96; owned by Dutch Intercoin Co.; "licenses in various countries"
Club Colonial	Costa Rica www.cccsportsbook.com	yes	
Club Rio Casino	Venezuela www.clubrio.com	yes	owner is Starnet International (Canada); uses EFS Caribbean equipment
Constellation Casino	Antigua www.virtcasino.com	n.a.	supplied by Virtual Gambling Technologies through its Antigua branch; sportsbook phase is International Sports Market (q.v.)

COMPANY	LOCATION	LICENSE?	COMMENTS
Country Club Casino	Tasmania www.murchison.com.au	yes	owned by Federal Hotels of Australia
Cowboy Casino	Antigua www.cowboycasino.com	yes	one of seven casinos using software from Bossmedia of Sweden, via Global Network Ltd., licensee
Cryatal Palace	Trinidad (no website found)	n.a.	under Casino Fortune group (Sunny Group)
Cyberbetz	Dominica www.cyberbetz.com	yes	owned by Global Intertainment Corp. of Vancouver; est. 8.98 after purchase of Netbetz; casino and sportsbook
Cyberbookies	Netherlands Antilles www.cyberbookies.com	n.a.	connected with Casino Café
CyberSino	Netherlands Antilles www.cybersino.com	n.a.	owned by Scylinx Corp. of Netherlands Antilles
Cyberspades	(location unknown) www.cyberspades.com	n.a.	
Cyber Thrill	Bahamas www.cyberthrill.com	n.a.	
Darwin All Sports	Darwin, Australia www.betthe.net	yes	est. Jan. 1997; is Internetarm of International All Sports, advertised as Australia's largest independent bookmaker; onto Internet 6/98; reportedly doing US$1 million per month of business 1998
Davidson Sports Betting	Sydney, Australia www.sportsbetting.aust.com	yes	est. July 1997; will go online only when New South Wales adopts regulation laws
Dial-a-Bet	Dominican Republic	out of business 1998	
Diamond Club Casino	Antigua www.diamondclub.com	yes	one of seven casinos using software of Bossmedia of Sweden, via Global Network, Ltd., licensee
Emerald Palms Sportsbook	Costa Rica www.epalms.com	yes	
English Harbour Casino Online	Antigua www.englishharbour.com	yes	owned by English Harbour Entertainment, Antigua
English Sports Betting	Jamaica and Antigua	no	on Antigua's "no license" list 1998; site says betting illegal for U.S. customers

COMPANY	LOCATION	LICENSE?	COMMENTS
Eurobet Sports	Gibraltar www.eurobet.com	yes	only customers outside U.K.; very primitive site
First Live Casino	St. Vincent www.firstlive.com	n.a.	roulette only
Five Star Casino	Antigua www.fivestar.com	yes	one of seven casinos using software from Bossmedia of Sweden, via Global Network, Ltd., licensee
Galaxiworld	St. Kitts www.galaxiworld.com	yes	owned by Gaming Lotteries Communication Ltd. (GLC Ltd.); est. 12/98; reported wagers US$3.1 million that month
Galaxy Sports and Casino	Curaçao	yes	prosecuted in New York federal case, 1998; bought 1998 by "group of international investors," including Royal Technologies telecom company; renamed operation Royal Sports
Gamblers Palace	Costa Rica www.gamblerspalace.com	yes	est. 8/98; casino and sportsbook
Gibraltar Sports	St. Kitts (no website found)	yes	owned by Gibraltar Sports, Inc.; spokesman: "There's no safety on the Internet; we don't do anything on it at all."
Global Casino	Grenada	out of business	owned by Michael Simone of Pennsylvania; out of business after Missouri civil and criminal cases of 1997; sold to International Gaming of Vancouver, 12/97
Global Sports Connection	Costa Rica www.betmaker.com	yes	prosecuted and pled guilty in New York federal case, 1998
Global SportsNet	Antigua (no website found)	no	specifically named as unlicensed in 1998 Antigua list of licensees
Gold Club Casinos	Antigua www.goldclubcasino.com	yes	one of seven casinos licensed to Global Network Inc., using software of Bossmedia of Sweden; probably sublicensing to many other casinos in Antigua
Gold Coast	Curaçao www.gcibet2.com	yes	also called Goldcoast Race and Sportsbook
Golden Hollywood Casino	Dominican Republic www.goldenhollywood.com	yes	est. October 1998
Golden Jackpot	Venezuela www.goldenjackpot.com	yes	licensee is U.S. Sports Casino; lists winners in U.S., but says play only allowed in "your particular state"; English and German

COMPANY	LOCATION	LICENSE?	COMMENTS
Golden Palace Casino	Antigua www.goldenpalace.com	yes	links connect with Nierfeld's Internet Casino (q.v.); "Golden Palace Group," all in Antigua, includes 28 casinos; wholly owned by Antiguan company
Grand Dominican Casino	Dominican Republic www.granddominican.com	yes	est. 9/97; active with U.S. customers, run by Tecnologia Co., headed by Joseph Tedeschi and group
Grand Holiday Casino	Curaçao (no website found)	out of business	
Grand Online Casino	Antigua www.grandonline.com	yes	connected with Triple Win Casino (q.v.)
Grand Prix Sportsbook and Casino	Costa Rica www.casino.grandprixsports.com	yes	developed by CyberRoad of Canada; has EBanx e-cash system
Grand Riviera	Antigua www.grandriviera.com	yes	under same management as Triple Win and about 25 other sites; a "private company" that would not divulge its name
Grand Towers	(location unknown) www.grandtowers.com	n.a.	
Inet Sportsbook	Costa Rica www.inetsportsbook.com	yes	also called Sports Bettor's Paradise; est. 1996
InterBingo	Gibraltar (no website found)	yes	associated with InterKeno, under NetGame, Ltd.
Intercasino	Antigua www.intercasino.com	yes	under WWTS group; est. 1996; offers 19 games
InterKeno	Gibraltar (no website found)	yes	InterKeno was former name of Casares (q.v.) --current association unknown
InterLotto	Liechtenstein www.interlotto.li	yes	direct government sanction; run by International Lottery in Liechtenstein Foundation; also known as Millions 2000
International Action Sports	St. Kitts www.international-action.com	yes	
International Sports Market	Antigua www.virtsports.com	yes	sportsbook phase of Constellation Casino; six languages
Intertops	Antigua www.intertops.com	yes	est. 1997; based in Austria;

COMPANY	LOCATION	LICENSE?	COMMENTS
Interwetten	Austria www.interwetten.com	yes	est. 1989 as phone-betting op.; online in 1997; in Vienna; advertises tax-free winnings, targeting Americans
Island Casino	Costa Rica (no website found)	out of business	
Island Sports	Curaçao (no website found)	n.a.	under new management 6/98
Island Superbook	St. Kitts	yes	bought 6/98 by Gibraltar Sports
Jackpot Palace	Antigua www.jackpotpalace.com	n.a.	advertised as coming in 1999; licensed to Global Network Ltd.; using software of Bossmedia of Sweden
Jupiters Casino	Australia www.broflo.com.au	yes	conventional casino, Conrad Jupiter's Gold Casino on Queensland's Gold Coast, purchased Centrebet 1998 and went online for first time, excluding U.S. customers
The King's Casino	Botswana (no website found)	n.a.	under Casino Fortune group based in Trinidad (Sunny Group)
Kings Casino	Antigua www.kingscasino.com	n.a.	no relation to Botswana operation
King's Sportsbook	Grenada	out of business	
Ladbroke's	United Kingdom (no website found)	yes	a top telephone bookmaker; no reported Internat operations but does have U.S. customers and is potential Internet operation
Lasseter's	Australis (no website found)	yes	conventional casino; reportedly will go online second half of 1999 from Alice Springs, Northern Terr.
Las Vegas Sportsbook	Dominican Republic (no website found)	n.a.	
Loose Lines	Margarita Island (Venezuela) www.looselines.com	yes	advertises that its location makes betting legal for all
Majestic Sports	Costa Rica (no website found)	n.a.	

COMPANY	LOCATION	LICENSE?	COMMENTS
Mapau Casino	Trinidad www.mapau.com	yes	in Casino Fortune group (Sunny Group)
Megasports	Antigua (no website found)	n.a.	website not complete 3/99; advertising for U.S. customers; Megasports also now has Australian site at www.megasports.com.au
Millions 2000 (see InterLotto)			
NASA Sportsbook	Costa Rica www.betonsports.com	yes	moved from Antigua 1998
NetBet (see Sportingbet)			
Netbetz	Dominica	yes	bought 1998 by Global Intertainment Corp.; name changed to Cyberbetz
New York Casino	Antigua www.newyorkcasino.com	yes	licensed to Global Network, Ltd., using software of Bossmedia of Sweden
Nierfeld's Internet Casino	Germany www.nierfeld.com	n.a.	claims to be first Internet casino in Germany, but German law does not permit Internet gaming; location unknown
Oasis Casino	Curaçao www.oasiscasino.com	n.a.	
Olympic Sportsbook	Jamaica www.thegreek.com	n.a.	
Omni Casino	Antigua www.omnicasino.com	yes	also known as Omni of the Caribbbean; in WWTS group; claims Antigua license puts it outside U.S. jurisdiction; est. 8/97
123 Casino	Grenada www.123casino.com	yes	casino and sportsbook; est. 6/97; site says Indiana and Missouri residents have been warned of betting illegality
Online Sports Bet	Costa Rica (no website found)	n.a.	
Paradise Sports	St. Kitts www.paradisesports.com	yes	uses Carib F/X software

COMPANY	LOCATION	LICENSE?	COMMENTS
Paradise Sportsbook	Costa Rica www.paradisesportsbook.com	n.a.	
Parlay Teaser	Costa Rica parlayteaser.com [sic]	n.a.	
Planet Poker	location unknown www.planetpoker.com	n.a.	"abides by all rules and regulations of the jurisdictions in which it operates," i.e., specifically refuses to identify location
Playboy Sportsbook	Costa Rica www.playboysportsbook.com	n.a.	est. 1996
Players Casino and Ssportsbook	has several casinos with ISPs in Caribbean -- no specific location found www.playersonly.com	n.a.	
Post Time Sports	Antigua ww.post-time.com	yes	est. 1996; affiliated with Bettorsworld listing service
Premier League	Antigua www.premierleague.com	n.a.	est. 1998
Queens Club Casino	Antigua (no website found)	n.a.	advertised as coming in 1999; licensed to Global Network Ltd., with software from Bossmedia of Sweden
Quick Pay Sports	Costa Rica www.quickpay.com	n.a.	
RKR Sports	Curaçao (no website found)	out of business	affiliated with Gold Coast and Top Turf; all gone by 1998
RYO International	Antigua www.twinklingstar.com	yes	casisno and sportsbook; est 1997
Ramses Valley of the Kings Casino	Antigua www.thevalleyofkings.com	n.a.	member of Golden Palace (q.v.) Group
Real Casino	Costa Rica (no website found)	n.a.	customer list purchased 1998 by Cyberbetz
Rich's Sportsbook	Dominican Republic (no website found)	out of business 1998	

COMPANY	LOCATION	LICENSE?	COMMENTS
Ritz Casino	Trinidad www.theritzcasino.com	yes	one of five under Casino Fortune, Sunny Group
Riviera Casinos	location unknown www.rivieracasinos.com	n.a.	English and German versions
Rosie's Casino	Costa Rica www.rosiescasino.com	yes	also known as Rosie's Chalk Garden Casino
Royal Island Casino and Sportsbook	Costa Rica [possible] www.royalisland.com	n.a.	est. 8/98, possibly as a new version of Island Casino
Royal St. Kitts Hotel and Casino	St. Kitts www.royalstkitts.com	yes	standard hotel casino for 15 years
Royal Sports	Curaçao www.royalsports.com	yes	new name of Galaxy Sports; bought by international group headed by Royal Technologies telecom company
SBG Global	Costa Rica www.sbgglobal.com	n.a.	
Safari International	Antigua www.safari-casino.com	yes	est. 1997
Sands of the Caribbean	Antigua www.thesands.com	yes	under WWTS group
7by7 Casino	location unknown www.7by7.com	n.a.	English and Japanese
Shamrock Sportsbook	Costa Rica www.shamrock.com	n.a.	
ShoreBet Sportsbook	Dominica www.shorebet.net	yes	est. 8/98
Skybook	Margarita Island (Venezuela) www.skybook.com	yes	Las Vegas-owned
Specfund	Antigua (no website found)	yes	

COMPANY	LOCATION	LICENSE?	COMMENTS
Specfund	Antigua (no website found)	yes	est. 1998
Sport Fanatik	Venezuela	yes	ten languages; uses EFS Caribbean software; sportsbook and casino
Sportbet.com	Costa Rica www.sportbet.com	n.a.	
Sportingbet.com	United Kingdom (Alderney Isl.) www.sportingbet.com	yes	run by Blandford Betting; established conventional bookmakers in England for 14 years
Sports Bettor's Paradise	Costa Rica www.inetsportsbook.com	yes	also known as Inetsportsbook; est. 1996
Sports Interaction	Dominican Republic (no website found)	out of business	money transactions reportedly went to Ireland
Sports International	Antigua/Grenada www.gamblenet.com	no	listed by Antigua on "no license" list 5/98
Sports Market	Curaçao www.sportsmarket.com (site "under construction")	n.a.	
Sports Net Bet	Costa Rica www.sportsnetbet.com	yes	est. 1996
Sports Offshore	Antigua www.sportsoffshore.com	yes	also known as SOS
Sports State	Curaçao (website temporarily down)	n.a.	
Sterling Sportsbook	Dominican Republic www.wagepage.com	yes	
Sunrise Casino	(location unknown) www.casino-sunrise.com	n.a.	uses Alesco Ltd. software
Sunset Casino	Antigua (no website found)	yes	advertised as coming in 1999; licensed to Global Network Ltd.; using software from Bossmedia of Sweden

COMPANY	LOCATION	LICENSE?	COMMENTS
Super Casino	Dominica www.supercasino.com	yes	links also go to Casino Casino; run by Super Casino, Ltd.
Superbet	Venezuela www.superbet.com	yes	est. 6/98
TABCORP	Victoria, Australia (no website found)	yes	formed 1994 by privatization of Victoria Totalizer Agency Board (TAB), which ran off track race betting for the govenment; may move to Internet soon (New South Wales's TAB went online early in 1999)
TVCCasino	Costa Rica www.tvccasino.com	n.a.	est 8/97; parent company is Lucheafar (Dutch); also sportsbook
Triple Win	Antigua www.triplewin.com	yes	under Gold Club Casino group
USA Casino	Antigua www.usacasino.com	yes	licensed to Global Network Ltd.; using software from Bossmedia of Sweden
Ultimate Sports Betting	Costa Rica www.ultimatesportsbetting.com	yes	est. 1/97
Universal Sportsbook	Dominican Republic (no website found)	n.a.	
VIP Sports	Netherlands Antilles www.vipsports.com	yes	
Victor Chandler	United Kingdom www.victorchandler.com	yes; Gibraltar	long-time conventional bookmaker in England, with offices in Hong Kong, Thailand, Gibraltar; recently into Internet; moving into U.S. market
Virtual Casino Online	Antigua www.virtcasino.com	yes	run by Virtual Gambling Technologies, Inc. through Antigua subsidiary; also runs Constellation Casino and its International Sports Market sportsbook
Wagersports	Bahamas (no website found)	out of business	
Wall Street Casino	Dominican Republic www.wallstreet-casino.com	yes	est. 8/98 "licensed and audited"

COMPANY	LOCATION	LICENSE?	COMMENTS
William Hill	United Kingdom (Isle of Man) www.williamhill.co.im	yes	conventional bookmaker since 1934; high reputation; recently into Internet
Wild West Frontier Casino	St. Kitts www.wildwestfrontier.com	n.a.	new 3/99; run by International Gaming, Ltd.; "100 percent European owned"
Winner's Way	Dominican Republic (no website found)	out of business?	target of 3/98 New York prosecution; owner pled guilty; website "removed for nonpayment"
Wizard of Odds	Dominical Republic www.wizardofodds.net	yes	est. 1998
World Sportsbook	Antigua www.worldsportsbook.com	yes	subsidiary of Starnet Communications International of Vancouver
World Sports Exchange	Antigua www.wsex.com	yes	target of 3/98 New York prosecution; owner Jay Cohen has fought the case
World-Wide Telesports (WWTS)	Antigua www.wwts.com	yes	target of 3/98 New York prosecution; owners charged but remain fugitives; sublicense numerous other operations; had prior solid reputation; software from Microgaming Systems Inc.
World Wide Wagering	Dominica www.wager.dm	yes	sportsbook and casino
World Wide Web Casinos	Antigua (no website found)	no	Antigua lists as not licensed; based in Orange County, CA; owns conventional casino, St. James Club, in Antigua
Wrest Point Casino	Tasmania (no website found)	yes	owned by Federal Hotals of Australia

APPENDIX I

COMPANIES RELATED TO INTERNET GAMING OPERATIONS

AMERICAN WAGERING, INC.—
Bookmaking company in Las Vegas and owner of Megasports, which has a casino in Antigua; opened Internet wagering operations in Canberra, early 1999, under license from the Australian Capital Territory, in partnership with Australian firm AWA of Sydney, a gambling group so far frustrated by New South Wales's failure to legalize gaming in its jurisdiction; Internet name will be Megasports.

ATLANTIC INTERNATIONAL ENTERTAINMENT, LTD.—Developer of Internet games and parent company of World Interactive Gaming Corp. of Delaware and New York, which was sued in 1998 by the Federal Trade Commission for illegal solicitation of investors in its Golden Chips Internet Casino, and by the State of New York for running an illegal Internet casino, also the Golden Chips Casino.

ATLANTIS GAMING, INC.— Recipient of first license from Softec Systems Caribbean, subsidiary of Starnet Communications International; has gaming licenses in Antigua and operates CasinoLand; formerly owned Atlantis Casino in Belize.

AUSTRALIAN MEDIA, LTD.—Owns exclusive franchise for online gaming on Norfolk Island, Australia, and uses software from New Discoveries (U.S.); ownership of Australian Media unknown.

BOSSMEDIA—Swedish firm running six casinos (soon to be nine, per advertising), in Antigua; licensed to Global Network Ltd.; two branch companies in Antigua—Boss Casinos and Webdollar—employing 50 people altogether.

COMMERCE AND COMMUNICATIONS INC.— In Antigua, mainly a software provider; has Antigua license for Internet gaming as of 1998.

CRYPTOLOGIC— Software development company based in Toronto; operator of virtual casinos; developed an e-cash system in which players establish accounts via credit card, check, money order, or wire, with encrypted financial information. Its casino system, Intercasino, was sold to its subsidiary Intertainment Antigua, which licensed it to World Wide Telesports (WWTS), Antigua, with all bets received, processed, and stored in Antigua. WWTS uses Cryptologic's e-cash for secure money transactions.

CYBEROAD GAMING CORPORATION—
Vancouver; owns or supplies operations in St. Kitts and Costa Rica.

CYBERGAMES— Costa Rica; runs Bingo of the Americas under contract with the Red Cross of the Americas, and also five casinos in Dominica and Antigua, purchased in 1998; development agreements with three other casinos and four conventional casinos in Costa Rica. Until 1998, called Professional Sports Holdings, Inc. Runs its Costa Rica sites through RCI de Costa Rica, SA.

CYBER SPACE CASINO TECH, LTD.— Location unknown; specializes in Internet gaming; works with Carib F/X and other software suppliers.

ELECTRONIC FINANCIAL SERVICES (EFS) CARIBBEAN— Provider of encryption and processing systems for financial transactions security, using STAR-MX software, to Internet gaming operations; calls itself an "international currency converter and secure Internet transaction gateway."

GLOBAL INTERTAINMENT INC.— Vancouver and Hong Kong; no U.S. citizens as principles; market focus Asia and Europe. Owner of Cyberbetz Internet gaming operation, Dominica.

INATOS, LTD.— Advertises as lowest-cost Internet service provider in Great Britain; designed Stopwatch Internet soccer betting site.

INTERACTIVE GAMING AND COMMUNICATIONS— Operated through Grenadian subsidiary, Global Casinos, beginning February 1997. Also ran WiseGuy Sports Wagering System, Global Casino, and Sports International, all in Grenada. Reported 1996 turnover was US$58.6 million. Brought to court in Missouri in 1997; owner Michael Simone sold the company to International Gaming Corp. of Vancouver, December 1997.

MEGASPORTS— Division of American Wagering, Inc.; in mid-1998 received Australian license in Canberra and plans to base new international operations in Australia

NTN GROUP— Australia; newly formed (2/99) company to develop, market, and operate gaming systems of the Australian Internet Gaming Company Coms21; shape and activity still to be determined.

NETGAME, LTD.—Gibraltar; operates (operated?) InterKeno and InterBingo

PAN INTERNATIONAL GAMING— Seattle; owns Tropical International Sports of Antigua (q.v.)

STARNET COMMUNICATIONS INTERNATIONAL— Founded 1995; Antigua-based; called "the Microsoft of casino software vendors"; has numerous gaming subsidiaries, including World Sportsbook, World Lotteries, World Racetracks, World Gaming Casino; online revenues processed through Electronic Financial Services Caribbean, based in Antigua, using technology from another branch, Starnet Canada. Electronic commerce certified by Bank of Montreal. Another subsidiary, Softec Systems Caribbean, licenses turnkey customized Internet gaming systems, including that of Atlantis Gaming Inc. of Antigua, operator of CasinoLand.

TELECOMMUNICATIONS INFRASTRUCTURE SUPPORT SERVICES (TISS)— Long Beach, CA, provides turnkey systems and consultation for casino sites and software; until 1998 owned Sports Market gaming site, Curaçao.

TROPICAL INTERNATIONAL SPORTS— Antigua, through Whitfield Holdings of Antigua, leases hardware and software from PAN International (q.v.); until sometime in 1998, was called RSB and was based in Dominica.

SOURCES

Electronic Cash

Ashworth, Jerry. 'Researcher's Smart Card Attack Discovery Spurs Industry to Search for Fixes to System, "<u>Report on Smart Cards</u>, 12, No. 13, July 20, 1998, 3-4.

Bielski, Lauren. 'Smart Cards, Coming Up to Bat, "<u>ABA Banking Journal</u>, 90, No. 11, November 1998, 67-68.

European Commission. 'Money Laundering: EU Directive to Be Extended "(July 13, 1998). European Union website: www.europa.eu.int.

European Commission. 'Electronic Money: Commission Proposes Clear Regulatory Framework "(July 29, 1998). European Union website: europa.eu.int.

'Financial Action Task Force on Money Laundering, "<u>The Forty Recommendations of the Financial Action Task Force on Money Laundering</u>. Paris: FATF Secretariat, OECD, June 28, 1996.

'Financial Action Task Force on Money Laundering, "<u>FATF Annexes: Annual Report, 1997-1998 (June 1998)</u>. Paris: FATF Secretariat, OECD, June 1998.

'Financial Action Task Force on Money Laundering, "<u>FATF 1998-1999 Report on Money Laundering Typolgies</u>. Paris: FATF Secretariat, OECD, February 10, 1999.

'Forrester Study Reassesses Smart Card Use in N. America, "<u>Report on Smart Cards</u>, 12, No. 3, February 16, 1998, 3-5.

Frost and Sullivan, 'The World Market in Review [1999]. " <http://www.smartcardcentral.com>

Guthrey, Scott B. 'Smart Cards in Web-Based E-Commerce. "Pages 137-67 in Mary J. Cronin, ed., <u>Banking and Finance on the Internet</u>. New York: Van Nostrand Reinhold, 1997.

Hendry, Mike. <u>Smart Card Security and Applications</u>. Boston: Artech House, 1997.

'Industry Analysis Firm Predicts 38 Percent Annual Growth in Smart Card Market, " <u>Report on Smart Cards</u>, 12, No. 2, February 2, 1998, 1-2, 11.

Richards, James R. <u>Transnational Criminal Organizations, Cybercrime, and Money Laundering</u>. Boca Raton: CRC Press, 1999.

<u>Smart Card Directory, 1999: A Comprehensive Worldwide Guide to Smart Card Projects, People, and Companies</u>. New York: Faulkner & Gray, 1998.

Yamaguchi, Mitsuo, et al. <u>Electronic Money: Its Impact on Retail Banking and Electronic Commerce</u>. Tokyo: F.I.A. Financial Publishing Co., 1997.

Websites:
    http://www.cybercash.com.
    http://www.digicash.com.
    http://www.europa.eu.int. [European Union]
    http://www.mondex.com.
    http://www.protonworld.com.
    http://www.smartcardcentral.com
    htto://www.smartcardforum.org.
    http://www.scia.org. [Smart Card Industry Association]
    http://www.treas.gov.
    http://www.visa.com.

Various issues of the following publications were also used in the preparation of this report: <u>Report on Smart Cards</u> [Washington, D.C.], and <u>Card Technology</u> [New York].

Electronic Banking

"ACI, Edify Partner to Provide Internet Banking Systems, "<u>Electronic Banker</u>, March 17, 1999. <http://www.electronicbanker.com/html/news/031799_2.htm>

"Announcement, "March 20, 1995. <http://virtualschool.edu/mon/ElectronicProperty/FBOIInfo>

Ashworth, Jerry. "SET's Future in Doubt as Banks Assess Protocols, "<u>Report on Smart Cards,</u> 12, No. 19, October 12, 1998, 5-6.

"Bankers Back Two Alternatives to Tellers: Internet and ATMs, "<u>GT Online: Industries</u>. <u>Currency</u>, 11, No. 1, Spring 1998. <http://www.GrantThornton.com/gtonline/finance/currency/sp98b.html>

"Banks Can No Longer Ignore the Internet, "<u>Bank Investment Services Report,</u> 7, No. 2, January 11, 1999, 5.

Blum, Jack A. <u>Enterprise Crime: Financial Fraud in International Interspace</u>. U.S. Working Group on Organized Crime. WGOC Monograph Series. Washington, DC: National Strategy Information Center, June 1997.

Chase, Brett. "Bank One CEO Bets $500M on Internet's Sales Potential, " <u>American Banker,</u>164, No. 34, February 22, 1999, 5.

Community Banks: A Competitive Force. 1999 Sixth Annual Survey of
        Community Bank Executives.
            <http://www.GrantThornton.com/gtonline/finance/banksurvey99/survey99w.html>

'Consortium Plans Cyberbank System."
            <http://www.cnnfn.com/archive/news/9605/14/nationsbank/index.htm>

Cordell, Arthur J. 'Nothing Fails Like Success: Online Growth in the Offshore World,"
        Journal of Internet Banking and Commerce [online].
            <http://www.arraydev.com/commerce/JIBC/9806-08.htm>

Cronin, Mary J., ed. Banking and Finance on the Internet. New York: Van Nostrand
        Reinhold, 1997.

Cuevas, Jackie. "The Internet Banking Horizon: Bleak or Bright for Community Banks?"
            <http://www.arraydev.com/commerce/JIBC/9811-14.htm>

'Customers Flock to New Internet Banking Business in Britain, "Evening Standard
        [London], January 19, 1999.

Dannenberg, Marius, and Dorothée Kellner. "The Bank of Tomorrow with Today's
        Technology, "International Journal of Bank Marketing [Bradford], 16, No. 2, 1998, 90-97.

'Deutsche Breathes Life into Retail, "Retail Banker International, No. 406,
        February 18, 1999, 7.

The Dominion of Melchizedek. <http://www.melchizedek.com> [homepage]

The Dominion of Melchizedek. 'Banking Act of 1991."
            <http://www.melchizedek.com/gvmtdocs/banking.htm>

'Eastern Bank Introduces Internet Banking Services in Effort to Reduce Costs and Compete
        with Local Online Banks, "Financial NetNews, 4, No. 4, January 25, 1999, 4.

Egland, Kori L., Karen Furst, Daniel E. Nolle, and Douglas Robertson, 'Banking over the
        Internet, "Quarterly Journal (Office of the Comptroller of the Currency), 17, No. 4,
        December 1998, 25-30.

'E*Offering Rattles I-Banking: Upstart Investment Bank Believes It Can Cut the
        Underwriting Fee on IPOs, "January 28, 1999.
            <http://www.cnnfn.com/digitaljam/redherring/9901/28/redherring_eoffering/>

'E*Trade, BofA and Visa to Offer Wireless Web Access Via PalmPilot, "FutureBanker, 3, No. 2,
        February 1999, 27.

'E*Trade Breaks New Investment Ground with Investment Bank, "January 20, 1999.
<http://www.cnnfn.com/digitaljam/newsbytes/124330.html>

'Europe's Banks Trying To Relate, "<u>Electronic Banker</u>, March 18, 1999.
<http://www.electronicbanker.com/html/news/031800_3.htm>

<u>Federal Register</u>, 63, No. 156, 43327-30, August 13, 1998. (Department of the Treasury.
Office of Thrift Supervision. 12 CFR Part 555, No. 98-77, RIN 1550-AB00).

<u>Federal Register</u>, 63, No. 229, 65673-83, November 30, 1998.

'Financial Action Task Force on Money Laundering, "<u>1998-1999 Report on Money
Laundering Typologie.</u> FATF Secretariat. Paris: February 10, 1999.

'Financial Action Task Force on Money Laundering Issues a Warning about Austrian
Anonymous Savings Passbooks, "February 11, 1999.
<http://www.oecd.org/fatf/Press%20Releases/Current/nw99-15a.htm> [news release]

'Financial Service Act Tackling Internet Banking, "<u>Electronic Banker</u>, March 15, 1999.
<http://www.electronicbanker.com/html/news/031599_5.htm>

Fisse, Brent, and Peter Leonard. 'International Electronic Money Systems and Money Laundering. "
Paper presented at ASC Electronic Commerce Conference, Sydney, Australia,
February 4, 1997.
<http://www.gtlaw.com.au/gt/pubs/moneylaundering.html#Heading1>

Furst, Karen, William W. Lang, and Daniel E. Nolle. "Technological Innovation in Banking and
Payments: Industry Trends and Implications for Banks, "<u>Quarterly Journal</u> (Office of the
Comptroller of the Currency), 17, No. 3 September 1998, 23-31.

'Gomez: Security First Is No. 1, Again, "<u>Electronic Banker</u>, March 18, 1999.
<http://www.electronicbanker.com/html/news/031899_2.htm>

Hampton, Mark. <u>The Offshore Interface: Tax Havens in the Global Economy</u>.
New York: St. Martin's Press, 1996.

Hitachi Research Institute. <u>Electronic Money: Its Impact on Retail Banking and\
Electronic Commerce</u>. Tokyo: F.I.A. Financial Publishing, 1997.

Hong Kong Monetary Authority. 'Security of Banking Transactions over the Internet, "
November 25, 1997.

'Hong Kong— Online Banking with Standard Chartered Bank, "March 24, 1998.
<http://www.cnnfn.com/digitaljam/newsbytes/109566.html>
<http://www.info.gov.hk/hkmaeng/bank>

Inside Fraud Bulletin [London], No. 3, October 1998.

Institute of International Bankers. Global Survey of Regulatory and Market Developments in
    Banking, Securities and Insurance. 1998. <http://www.iib.org/global/1998>

International Finance and Commodities Institute. "Annex C: Offshore Group of Banking
    Supervisors: On-site Examination Checklist, "The Supervision of Cross-Border Banking.
    Committees at the Bank for International Settlement: May 15, 1995.
    <http://risk.ifci.ch/136260.htm>

"Internet Banking in Europe. "
    <http://www.internet-banking.com/barometer/barometerpage.html>

"Internet Banking and Shopping: Cyber-Buyer Beware, "FDIC Consumer News, Fall 1997.
    <http://www.fdic.gov/consumer/consnews/fal97/netbank.html>

"Internet Security System Launched, "Regulatory Compliance Watch, 9, No. 43,
    November 9, 1998, 1.

"JETCO Becomes Hong Kong's First Certified Internet Bank, " Newsbytes News Network.
    March 8, 1999. <http://www.newsbytes.com>

"Kentucky Gets Full-Service Internet Bank, "Lexington Herald-Leader, February 2, 1999, n.p.

"MAS 626-Notice to Banks, Banking Act, Cap 19, Guidelines on Prevention of Money Laundering, "
    Monetary Authority of Singapore, January 28, 1999. <http://www.mas.gov.sg>

Marjanovic, Steven. "A Week of Milestones for Security First, "American Banker, 164, No. 40,
    March 1, 1999, 17.

Marjanovic, Steven. "Web Bank's Revenue up 120% in Year, "American Banker Online,
    February 8, 1999. <http://www.tele-bank.com/media_ambank3.asp?>

McKegney, Margaret. "Credit Agricole to Link Web Banking to Satellite Service, "
    Financial NetNews, 3, No. 43, October 26, 1998, 1ff.

Molander, Roger C., David A. Mussington, and Peter A. Wilson. Cyberpayments and Money
    Laundering: Problems and Promise. Santa Monica: RAND Critical Technology
    Institute, 1998.

"Net banking services for Japan, "Reuters, special to CNET News.com, June 22, 1998.

"New Virtual Banks Coming Online, "Electronic Banker.
    <http://www.electronicbanker.com/html/news/020999_3.htm>

"Online Banking, "Bank Rate Monitor. <http://www.bankrate.com/brm/publ/onlifees.asp>

"Online Banking: New Internet Bank Looks to Stand Out from Crowd, "American Banker, 164, No. 32, February 18, 1999, 8.

Orr, Bill. "Community Guide to Internet Banking, "ABA Banking Journal. <http://www.banking.com/aba/feature_0698.asp>

"OTS Approves Internet Bank to Provide Range of Services, "OTS News Release, July 14, 1997, OTS97-44. <http://www.ots.treas.gov/docs/7744.html>

"OTS Updates Electronic Operations Rule to Help Thrifts Better Compete, "OTS 98-89, November 30, 1998. (Department of the Treasury. Office of Thrift Supervision. Transmittal TR-212.)

Potipattanakorn, Sompit. "Electronic Banking Comes to Thai Farmers Bank, "The Nation [Bangkok], October 6, 1998. <http://www.cnnfn.com/digitaljam/newsbytes/119206.html>

Power, Carol. "Chase, Playing Catch-Up, Adds Web Access to Its Online Banking Service, " American Banker, 164, No. 38, February 26, 1999, 10.

"Press Release, " [Bankruptcy Proceedings Initiated for Credit Bank and Roger Rosemont] September 3, 1998. <http://www.melchizedek.com/press/CreditBank.htm>

Richards, James R. Transnational Criminal Organizations, Cybercrime, and Money Laundering: A Handbook for Law Enforcement Officers, Auditors, and Financial Investigators. Boca Raton: CRC Press, 1999.

Risk Management for Electronic Banking and Electronic Money Activities. Basle: Basle Committee on Banking Supervision, March 1998.

Run, Benny. "Online Bank Transactions to Begin in Israel, "InternetNews.com, March 23, 1999. <http://www.internetnews.com/intl-news/article/0,1087,6_84871,00.html>

Samaad, Michelle. "A Window to the Bank That Never Closes, "Online Finance, Pt 2. <http://www.bankrate.com/brm/news/bank/19990302.asp>

Samaad, Michelle. "Big Names May Bring a Boost to Online Banking, "Bank Rate Monitor, September 29, 1998. <http://www.bankrate.com/brm/news/bank/19980929.asp>

Samaad, Michelle. "Cyber-Banking Breaks New Ground, Expands Toward Mainstream, " Bank Rate Monitor, January 12, 1999. <http://www.tele-bank.com/media_bank_monitor.asp?>

'Small-Fry Salem Five Cents Savings Masters Internet, "<u>FutureBanker</u>, 3, No. 2, February 1999, 43.

Sneddon, Mark. 'Cyberbanking: Remote Banking Using the Internet, "<u>Australian Business Law</u> <u>Review</u> [Sydney], 25, No. 1, February 1997, 64-67.

'TD to Offer Account Access in U.S. via Waterhouse, "<u>Financial NetNews</u>, 4, No. 4, January 25, 1999, 2.

'Testimony of James D. Kamihachi, Senior Deputy Comptroller for Economic and Policy Analysis, Office of the Comptroller of the Currency, Before the Subcommittee on Capital Markets, Securities and Government-Sponsored Enterprises of the Committee on Banking and Financial Services of the U.S. House of Representatives, "March 25, 1999.

'Thai Farmers Bank to Launch Internet Banking in Late 1998, "April 6, 1998. <http://www.cnnfn.com/digitaljam/newsbytes/110170.html>

'True U.S. Internet Banks, "<u>Online Banking Report</u>. Updated March 10, 1999. <http://www.onlinebankingreport.com/fullserv2.shtml>

'True World Internet Banks, "<u>Online Banking Report</u>. Updated March 10, 1999. <http://www.onlinebankingreport.com/fullserv_world_banks.shtml>

United States. Department of Treasury. Financial Crimes Enforcement Network. Office of International Programs. <u>Summary of FATF´s 1998-1999 Report on Money Laundering</u> <u>Typologies</u>. [also Annexes, via PDF file, Internet]

United States. General Accounting Office. <u>Report on Electronic Banking</u>. July, 1999.

'Viva La Internet Banking, "<u>Financial Service ONLINE</u>, January 1999, 6.

'Welcome to the Wonderful World of...Offshore Banking. " <http://www.offshoreprofit.un/op/043/banking/index.html>

'Wells Fargo Bank Eliminates Human Tellers in Trial, "November 6, 1998. <http://www.cnnfn.com/digitaljam/newsbytes/121028.html>

Yerkes, Leisha. 'Growing with Technology: The Benefits of Internet Banking, " <u>Bankinfo.com</u>, October 13, 1998. <http://www.bankino.com/ecomm/growing.html>

Numerous websites, particularly those belonging to banking institutions, regulatory agencies, and professional associations and journals, also were consulted.

http://www.banking.com/aba
http://www.bankrate.com
http://www.cnnfn.com
http://www.fdic.gov
http://GrantThornton.com/gtonline/
http://www.iib.org
http://www.internetnews.om
http://newsbytes.com
http://www.occ.gov
http://www.oecd.org/fatf
http://www.onlinebankingreport.com/fullserv
http://www.ots.treas.gov

Internet Gaming

Cabot, Anthony. <u>Internet Gaming Report II</u>. Las Vegas: Trace Publications, 1998.

Kelly, Joseph M., "Internet Gambling Law," 1999 draft of article for <u>Journal of Computer and Information Law</u>, v. 17, 1999 (forthcoming).

Rose, I. Nelson. <u>The Law of Internet Gambling</u>. (Manuscript), 1999.

Websites consulted:

http://www.bettorsworld.com
http://www.lotteryinsider.com.au
http://www.rgtonline.com (Rolling Good Times Online)

ENDNOTES

1 "More Consumers Bank on the Web, "The *Washington Post*, June 1, 1999, D1.

2 Scott B. Guthrey, "Smart Cards in Web-Based E-Commerce, "in Mary J. Cronin, ed., <u>Banking and Finance on the Internet</u> (New York: Van Nostrand Reinhold, 1997), 147; Mitsuo Yamaguchi et al., <u>Electronic Money: Its Impact on Retail Banking and Electronic Commerce</u> (Tokyo: F.I.A. Financial Publishing Co., 1997), 20-22.

3 See "Remarks by Eugene A. Ludwig, Comptroller of the Currency, "in conference entitled "Toward Electronic Money & Banking: The Role of Government, "September 19-20, 1996. http://www.occ.treas.gov/emoney/ludwig.html

4 "Industry Analysis Firm Predicts 38 Percent Annual Growth in Smart Card Market, "<u>Report on Smart Cards</u>, 12, No. 2 (February 2, 1998), 1-2, 11.

5 "Forrester Study Reassesses Smart Card Use in N. America, "<u>Report on Smart Cards</u>, 12, No. 3 (February 16, 1998), 3-5.

6 Frost & Sullivan, "The World Market in Review [1999], "and "A Look at the Asian Pacific Smart Cards Market: 1999 and Onwards. "http://www.smartcardcentral.com.

7 "Banks Can No Longer Ignore the Internet, "<u>Bank Investment Services Report</u>, 7, No. 2, January 11, 1999, 5.

8 James R. Richards, <u>Transnational Criminal Organizations, Cybercrime, and Money Laundering: A Handbook for Law Enforcement Officers, Auditors, and Financial Investigators</u> (Boca Raton: CRC Press, 1999), 66.

9 "Bank One CEO Bets $500M on Internet's Sales Potential, "<u>American Banker</u>, 164, No. 34, February 22, 1999, 5.

10 "Kentucky Gets Full-Service Internet Bank, "<u>Lexington Herald-Leader</u>, February 2, 1999, n.p.

11 <http://www.gomezwire.com/Finance/Banks/scorecard/index.cfm?cat=1>

12 "IDC Predicts Internet Banking Explosion. "<http://www.electronicbanker.com/html/news/020299_4.htm>.

13 Erika Morphy, "Making Cash Flow, "<u>Export Today</u>, July 1998, 28.

[14] Jackie Cuevas, "The Internet Banking Horizon: Bleak or Bright for Community Banks? " <u>Journal of Internet Banking and Commerce.</u> [online] <http://www.arraydev.com/commerce/JIBC/9811-14.htm.>; Leisha Yerkes, "Growing with Technology: The Benefits of Internet Banking, "<u>Bankinfo.com,</u> October 13, 1998 <http://www.bankinfo.com/ecomm/growing.html>; "Testimony of James D. Kamihachi.... "citing Stephen C. Franco and Timothy M. Klein, <u>1999 Online Banking Report</u>, and Piper Jaffray, February 1999, 23, who placed the cost of a customer transaction via a telephone call center at US$0.84. and the Internet cost at US$0.26.

[15] "Bankers Back Two Alternatives to Tellers: Internet and ATMs, "<u>GT Online: Industries.</u> [from <u>Currency</u>, 11, No. 1, Spring 1998; <http://www.GrantThornton.com/gtonline/finance/currency/sp98b.html>

[16] Institute of International Bankers. <u>Global Survey of Regulatory and Market Developments in Banking, Securities and Insurance.</u> <http://www.iib.org/global/1998>

[17] <u>Risk Management for Electronic Banking and Electronic Money Activities.</u> Basle, Basle Committee on Banking Supervision, March 1998.

[18] "Comments from the Board of Governors of the Federal Reserve System, " <u>Electronic Banking: Enhancing Federal Oversight of Internet Banking Activities.</u> GAO Report, July 1999, GAO/GGD-99-91, 41.

[19] <http://www.occ.treas.gov/customer.htm>

[20] "Rule to Let S&Ls Offer Services Electronically, "<u>Report on Smart Cards</u>, December 14, 1998, 8; <u>Federal Register</u>, 63, No. 156, 43327-30, August 13, 1998 (Department of the Treasury. Office of Thrift Supervision. 12 CFR Part 555, No. 98-77, RIN 1550-AB00); "OTS Updates Electronic Operations Rule to Help Thrifts Better Compete, "OTS 98-89, November 30, 1998; Department of the Treasury. Office of Thrift Supervision. Transmittal TR-212. <u>Federal Register</u>, 63, No. 229, 65673-83, November 30, 1998.

[21] General Accounting Office, <u>Electronic Banking: Enhancing Federal Oversight of Internet Banking Activities</u>. GAO Report, July 1999, GAO/GGD-99-91.

[22] "Announcement, "March 20, 1995. <http://virtualschool.edu/mon/ElectronicProperty/FBOIInfo>

[23] "State Business of Banking Laws and the Internet, "21st Century Banking Alert No. 97-9-10, September 10, 1997. <http://www.ffhsj.com/bancmail/21starch/970910.htm>

[24] "IDC Predicts Internet Banking Explosion, "<u>Electronic Banker.</u> <http://www.electronicbanker.com/html/news/020299_4.htm>

[25] States participating in FinCEN Survey: Alabama, Alaska, Arizona, California, Colorado, Georgia, Hawaii, Iowa, Maryland, Minnesota, Nebraska, Nevada, New Jersey, New York, Ohio, Oklahoma, Rhode Island, South Carolina, Tennessee.

[26] Lauren Bielski, "Smart Cards, Coming Up to Bat, "<u>ABA Banking Journal</u>, 90, No. 11 (November 1998), 67-69.

[27] Mike Hendry, Smart Card Security and Applications (Boston: Artech House, 1997), 67-69.

[28] Ibid., 75-77.

[29] Jerry Ashworth, 'Researchers 'Smart Card Attack Discovery Spurs Industry to Search for Fixes to Systems,"Report on Smart Cards, 12, No. 13 (July 20, 1998), 3.

[30] European Commission, 'Electronic Money: Commission Proposes Clear Regulatory Framework "(July 29, 1998). European Union website: <www.europa.eu.int>.

[31] Financial Action Task Force on Money Laundering, The Forty Recommendations of the Financial Action Task Force on Money Laundering (Paris: FATF Secretariat, OECD, June 28, 1996).

[32] Financial Action Task Force on Money Laundering, FATF Annexes: Annual Report, 1997-1998 (June 1998) (Paris: FATF Secretariat, OECD, June 1998); and Financial Action Task Force on Money Laundering, FATF 1998-1999 Report on Money Laundering Typologies (Paris: FATF Secretariat, OECD, February 1999).

[33] James R. Richards, Transnational Criminal Organizations, Cybercrime, and Money Laundering: A Handbook for Law Enforcement Officers, Auditors, and Financial Investigators (Boca Raton: CRC Press, 1999), 66.

[34] Richards, 66; 'OTS Approves Internet Bank to Provide Range of Services,"OTS News Release, July 14, 1997, OTS97-44. <http://www.ots.treas.gov/docs/7744.html>

[35] Michelle Samaad, 'Cyber-Banking Breaks New Ground, Expands Toward Mainstream, "Bank Rate Monitor, January 12, 1999. <http://www.tele-bank.com/media_bank_monitor.asp?>

[36] 'Wells Fargo Bank Eliminates Human Tellers in Trial, "November 6, 1998. <http://www.cnnfn.com/digitaljam/newsbytes/121028.html>

[37] 'New Virtual Banks Coming Online, "Electronic Banker. <http://www.electronicbanker.com/html/news/020999_3.htm>

[38] 'New Virtual Banks Coming Online, 'Electronic Banker. <http://www.electronicbanker.com/html/news/020999_3.htm>

[39] Marjanovic, Steven, 'Web Bank's Revenue up 120% in Year, "American Banker Online, February 8, 1999. <http://www.tele-bank.com/media_ambank3.asp?>

[40] Michelle Samaad, 'Cyber-Banking Breaks New Ground, Expands Toward Mainstream, "Bank Rate Monitor, January 12, 1999. <http://www.tele-bank.com/media_bank_monitor.asp?

[41] Carol Power, 'Chase, Playing Catch-UP, Adds Web Access to Its Online Banking Service, " American Banker, 164, No. 38, February 26, 1999, 10.

[42] 'Small-Fry Salem Five Cents Savings Masters Internet, "FutureBanker, 3, No. 2, February 1999, 43.

---

[43] 'E*Trade, BofA and Visa to Offer Wireless Web Access Via PalmPilot, "FutureBanker, 3, No. 2, February 1999, 27.

[44] 'Viva La Internet Banking, "Financial Service ONLINE, January 1999, 6.

[45] 'Deutsche Breathes Life into Retail, "Retail Banker International, No. 406, February 18, 1999, 7.

[46] Margaret McKegney, 'Credit Agricole to Link Web Banking to Satellite Service, "Financial NetNews, 3, No. 43, October 26, 1998, 1ff.

[47] 'Sweden No 1 in Internet banking, " <http://www.tagish.co.uk/ethosub/lit5/d842.htm>.

[48] 'Customers Flock to New Internet Banking Business in Britain, "Evening Standard [London], January 19, 1999.

[49] Benny Run, 'Online Bank Transactions to Begin in Israel, "InternetNews.com. March 23, 1999. <http://www.internetnews.com/intl-news/article/0,1087,6_84871,00.html>

[50] 'Southern Bank Direct. " <http://www.sbbgroup.com.my/sbbdirect/index.html>

[51] "Thai Farmers Bank to Launch Internet Banking in Late 1998, "April 6, 1998. <http://www.cnnfn.com/digitaljam/newsbytes/110170.html>

[52] Sompit Potipattanakorn, 'Electronic Banking Comes to Thai Farmers Bank, "The Nation [Bangkok], October 6, 1998. <http://www.cnnfn.com/digitaljam/newsbytes/119206.html>

[53] 'FATF-IX Report on Money Laundering Typologies, "February 12, 1998; 'Financial Action Task Force On Money Laundering, " 1998-1999 Report on Money Laundering Typologies. (Paris: FATF Secretariat), February 10, 1999.

[54] Current members of the Group are Aruba, Bahamas, Bahrain, Barbados, Bermuda, Cayman Islands, Cyprus, Gibraltar, Guernsey, Hong Kong, Isle of Man, Jersey, Lebanon, Malta, Mauritius, Netherlands Antilles, Panama, Singapore, and Vanuatu.

[55] Information was not available at the time of writing.

[56] Reference was made to the existence of the casino, but no website was located.

www.ingramcontent.com/pod-product-compliance
Lightning Source LLC
Chambersburg PA
CBHW080306290526
45790CB00005B/1949